AI & MOTOCROSS

Discover the Proven AI Strategies That Professional Riders Use to Dominate the Track and Crush the Competition

Chapter 1: The Evolution of Motocross and the Rise of AI

Section 1.1: The History of Motocross

- The Birth of Motocross: From its origins to modern racing.
- Key Technological Milestones in Motocross Equipment.
- Challenges Riders Faced Before the Digital Era.

Section 1.2: The Emergence of AI in Sports

- Defining AI and Its Capabilities.
- Examples of AI in Other Sports: Lessons for Motocross.
- The Potential of AI to Transform Motocross Racing.

Section 1.3: Why AI Matters in Motocross

- The Unique Demands of Motocross Racing.
- How AI Addresses Rider, Bike, and Track Challenges.
- The Future of AI and Motocross Synergy.

Chapter 2: AI-Powered Training for Riders

Section 2.1: Personalized Training Programs

- The Role of Wearables in Collecting Data.
- AI-Driven Fitness and Endurance Recommendations.
- Adapting Training Plans Based on Progress.

Section 2.2: Skill Development Through AI

- Analyzing Riding Techniques Using Machine Learning.
- Simulation Tools for Practicing in a Virtual Environment.
- Feedback Mechanisms for Real-Time Improvement.

Section 2.3: Mental Preparation Using AI Tools

- Using AI to Build Mental Resilience.
- Gamification Techniques for Training Motivation.
- Predictive Models for Stress and Fatigue Management.

Chapter 3: Optimizing Bike Performance with AI

Section 3.1: AI-Driven Diagnostics

- Using Sensors to Monitor Bike Health.
- Identifying Mechanical Issues Before They Occur.
- Preventative Maintenance Recommendations.

Section 3.2: Customizing Bikes for Peak Performance

- AI Tools for Optimizing Suspension and Tires.
- Adapting Engine Settings Based on Terrain Data.
- Predictive Adjustments for Weather and Track Conditions.

Section 3.3: Enhancing Safety Through AI

- Crash Prediction and Avoidance Systems.
- AI-Enabled Tools for Monitoring Rider Safety.
- Real-Time Alerts for Bike and Rider Risks.

Chapter 4: AI and Track Analysis

Section 4.1: Understanding Track Dynamics

- Using Drones and AI to Map Tracks.
- Collecting Data on Track Surface Variability.
- Visualizing Track Challenges Through AI Tools.

Section 4.2: Strategic Race Planning

- Predicting the Best Lines for Maximum Speed.
- Adapting Race Strategy Based on Competitor Data.
- Leveraging AI Insights for In-Race Adjustments.

Section 4.3: Post-Race Analytics

- Reviewing Performance Metrics After a Race.
- Identifying Areas for Improvement Using AI Reports.
- Applying Insights to the Next Race Plan.

Chapter 5: AI for Competitive Advantage

Section 5.1: Leveraging Data from Competitors

- AI Tools to Study Rival Performance.
- Gaining Insights into Competitor Weaknesses.
- Anticipating Opponent Strategies.

Section 5.2: AI in Team Collaboration

- Sharing Data Between Riders, Coaches, and Mechanics.
- Improving Communication Through AI-Powered Platforms.
- Coordinating Pit Stops Using AI Predictions.

Section 5.3: Staying Ahead with Cutting-Edge Tools

- Emerging AI Trends in Motocross.
- Investing in the Right AI Technology.
- Using AI to Maintain Long-Term Competitive Edges.

Chapter 6: AI in Event and Race Management

Section 6.1: Enhancing Event Logistics

- AI for Organizing Race Schedules and Timelines.
- Optimizing Rider and Team Accommodation.
- Real-Time Communication with Teams and Fans.

Section 6.2: Improving Audience Engagement

- AI-Driven Broadcasting and Commentary Enhancements.
- Virtual and Augmented Reality Experiences for Fans.
- Using AI to Build Interactive Fan Communities.

Section 6.3: Sustainability and Ethics in AI-Powered Events

- Reducing Environmental Impact with AI.
- Ethical Considerations in AI Usage.
- Ensuring Fair Competition Through AI Regulation.

Chapter 7: The Role of AI in Rider Safety and Injury Recovery

Section 7.1: AI for Preventing Injuries

- Monitoring Rider Fatigue with Wearable Tech.
- AI Alerts for Dangerous Riding Conditions.
- Adaptive Coaching for Minimizing Risk.

Section 7.2: Accelerating Injury Recovery

- AI-Assisted Physical Therapy Programs.
- Tracking Rehabilitation Progress with Data.
- Virtual Coaches for Recovery Motivation.

Section 7.3: Mental Health Support with AI

- Identifying Stress Levels Through Biometrics.
- AI Tools for Reducing Anxiety and Building Focus.
- Long-Term Mental Wellness Planning.

Chapter 8: The Future of AI in Motocross

Section 8.1: Innovations on the Horizon

- AI Advancements in Autonomous Bikes and Robotics.
- Integrating AI with Other Cutting-Edge Technologies.
- The Potential of AI in Motocross Coaching and Training.

Section 8.2: Preparing for the AI Revolution

- How Riders Can Embrace and Learn AI Tools.
- Opportunities for Teams to Invest in AI Research.
- Challenges and Solutions in Adopting AI at Scale.

Section 8.3: Vision for AI-Driven Motocross

- Reimagining the Motocross Experience for Riders and Fans.
- Creating a Collaborative AI Ecosystem in the Industry.
- Building the AI-Powered Motocross World of Tomorrow.

Introduction: The Intersection of Speed, Skill, and Intelligence

Motocross is more than a sport; it's a lifestyle, a community, and an art form. For decades, riders, teams, and engineers have worked tirelessly to push the boundaries of what's possible on the dirt track. From the roar of finely tuned engines to the thrill of mastering a challenging jump, motocross combines human skill, mechanical innovation, and sheer determination. Yet, like every other sport, motocross is now standing at the crossroads of a new revolution: the rise of artificial intelligence (AI).

In this book, *AI on the Track: Revolutionizing Motocross with Artificial Intelligence*, we'll explore how AI is reshaping the motocross world, providing riders and teams with unprecedented tools to enhance performance, optimize equipment, and dominate the track. This chapter sets the stage for the journey ahead by introducing the core themes of the book, outlining the transformative potential of AI in motocross, and giving you a glimpse of the benefits you can expect to unlock by leveraging this cutting-edge technology.

Motocross in the Age of Technology

Motocross, like all motorsports, has always relied on innovation. From lightweight materials and advanced suspension systems to precision-engineered engines, technological advancements have continually redefined what riders can achieve. However, despite these breakthroughs, motocross remains a sport where success depends on the perfect combination of human skill, machine performance, and environmental adaptation.

This is where AI enters the picture. Unlike traditional tools and techniques, AI goes beyond simply enhancing mechanical capabilities. It integrates data, machine learning, and predictive analytics to provide riders and teams with actionable insights that were previously unimaginable. Whether it's optimizing a bike's settings for a specific track, predicting maintenance needs, or helping a rider perfect their cornering technique, AI adds an entirely new dimension to motocross performance.

Why AI Matters in Motocross

The potential of AI in motocross can be summed up in one word: **optimization**. Every aspect of motocross—training, bike performance, track analysis, strategy, and safety—can be optimized with the help of AI. Let's break this down into three key areas:

1. Enhanced Rider Performance

AI has the power to revolutionize how riders train and perform. Through wearable sensors and advanced analytics, AI can track every detail of a rider's performance, from body positioning and acceleration to braking and cornering. By analyzing this data, AI tools can identify areas for improvement and provide tailored recommendations, enabling riders to train smarter, not harder.

Imagine an AI tool that notices you're losing valuable milliseconds on tight corners. It analyzes your body position, brake timing, and throttle control, then provides actionable feedback to help you shave seconds off your lap time. For professional riders, this kind of precision can mean the difference between winning and losing.

2. Smarter Bike Maintenance

Motocross bikes endure some of the harshest conditions in motorsports. The constant strain on engines, suspension, and tires makes maintenance both essential and challenging. AI simplifies this process by predicting when components are likely to fail and recommending maintenance schedules tailored to your bike's usage.

For example, an AI-powered diagnostic system could analyze engine performance data and alert you to a potential issue before it causes a breakdown during a race. This not only saves time and money but also ensures your bike is always in peak condition.

3. Strategic Race Planning

Motocross isn't just about raw speed—it's about strategy. From choosing the right lines on a track to adapting to changing weather conditions, the best riders are those who can think several steps ahead. AI excels at this kind of strategic thinking.

By analyzing track data, weather forecasts, and competitor performance, AI can help riders and teams develop winning strategies. It can identify the fastest lines, suggest optimal tire pressure for specific conditions, and even predict how competitors might perform based on past data. With AI, motocross becomes as much a game of intelligence as it is a test of skill and endurance.

Who This Book Is For

This book is designed for anyone who loves motocross and wants to understand how AI is changing the game. Whether you're a professional rider looking to gain a competitive edge, a hobbyist who wants to optimize your performance, or a team manager searching for innovative ways to support your riders, this book will provide you with the knowledge and tools you need to succeed.

Even if you're completely new to AI, don't worry. We'll start with the basics and gradually delve into more advanced concepts. Each chapter is packed with practical examples, step-by-step guides, and insights from industry leaders to help you apply AI effectively in your motocross journey.

The Structure of the Book

To help you navigate this exciting topic, we've divided the book into eight comprehensive chapters. Each chapter focuses on a specific aspect of motocross and AI, providing you with the tools and knowledge to transform how you approach the sport.

- **Chapter 1: The Evolution of Motocross and the Rise of AI** introduces the history of motocross, the basics of AI, and why these two fields are now intersecting.
- **Chapter 2: AI-Powered Training for Riders** explores how AI can enhance rider performance through personalized training programs, skill development tools, and mental preparation.
- **Chapter 3: Optimizing Bike Performance with AI** covers how AI can help you maintain, customize, and enhance your motocross bike for peak performance.
- **Chapter 4: AI and Track Analysis** dives into how AI tools can help you understand track dynamics, plan race strategies, and analyze post-race performance.
- **Chapter 5: AI for Competitive Advantage** focuses on using AI to study competitors, collaborate with teams, and stay ahead of the curve.
- **Chapter 6: AI in Event and Race Management** explores how AI is transforming motocross events, from logistics and broadcasting to audience engagement.
- **Chapter 7: The Role of AI in Rider Safety and Injury Recovery** discusses how AI can improve rider safety and accelerate recovery from injuries.
- **Chapter 8: The Future of AI in Motocross** looks ahead to the innovations and trends that will shape the future of motocross.

What You'll Gain from This Book

By the time you finish this book, you'll have a clear understanding of how AI is revolutionizing motocross and how you can leverage it to enhance your performance, improve your bike, and achieve your goals. You'll learn:

- How to use AI tools to analyze your riding technique and make targeted improvements.
- The best ways to optimize your bike's performance with AI-driven diagnostics and maintenance tools.
- How to develop smarter race strategies based on AI insights into track conditions and competitor data.
- Tips for using AI to stay safe, recover faster, and build long-term resilience as a rider.
- A roadmap for embracing the AI revolution and staying ahead of the competition.

A Call to Action

Motocross has always been about pushing limits—whether it's the limits of speed, endurance, or innovation. With AI, we have an opportunity to push those limits even further. This book is your guide to embracing the future of motocross, unlocking your full potential, and staying at the forefront of this exhilarating sport.

Are you ready to join the AI revolution and take your motocross journey to the next level? Let's get started.

Here's a detailed 8-chapter outline for *AI on the Track: Revolutionizing Motocross with Artificial Intelligence.*

Chapter 1: The Evolution of Motocross and the Rise of AI

Section 1.1: The History of Motocross

Motocross, a high-octane sport filled with adrenaline, skill, and grit, has a fascinating history. Its evolution from rudimentary off-road biking to the technologically advanced world we know today reflects humanity's constant push for innovation and thrill. This section explores motocross's origins, the technological advancements that shaped it, and the challenges riders faced before the digital age.

The Birth of Motocross: From Its Origins to Modern Racing

Motocross began in the early 20th century as a rugged test of endurance and skill. Rooted in the United Kingdom, the sport evolved from motorcycle trials, where riders navigated off-road terrain filled with natural obstacles like rocks, streams, and steep inclines. Unlike today's precision-engineered tracks, these early trials were raw and unpredictable, showcasing the rider's ingenuity as much as their bike's capabilities.

The first official motocross competition, known as a "scramble" at the time, took place in the 1920s. These events were informal and more about camaraderie and fun than structured competition. Riders often modified their motorcycles themselves, using ingenuity to adapt street bikes to the rigors of off-road racing. This early innovation paved the way for the sport's development.

By the 1930s, motocross gained popularity across Europe, with organized events becoming more competitive. The rugged terrain and unpredictable conditions of early courses demanded both physical and mental endurance from riders. Post-World War II saw motocross flourish as manufacturers like BSA, Norton, and Matchless entered the scene with specialized off-road bikes. The 1947 Motocross des Nations, held in the Netherlands, marked a pivotal moment, establishing motocross as an international sport.

The 1960s and 1970s brought motocross to the global stage. With the emergence of Japanese manufacturers like Honda, Suzuki, Yamaha, and Kawasaki, the sport underwent significant transformation. These companies introduced lighter, faster, and more reliable bikes, revolutionizing motocross. Tracks became more standardized, with jumps, berms, and other features designed to test skill and strategy. The rise of televised motocross events, especially in the United States, further catapulted the sport into mainstream popularity, giving rise to legends like Roger De Coster, the "Man of Motocross."

Key Technological Milestones in Motocross Equipment

As motocross evolved, so did the equipment that powered it. The technological milestones in bike design, safety gear, and track-building equipment have played a critical role in shaping the sport into what we see today.

1. The Shift to Lightweight Frames

Early motocross bikes were heavy and cumbersome, often modified from standard road bikes. The introduction of lightweight aluminum and chromoly steel frames in the 1970s revolutionized bike performance. These materials reduced weight while maintaining durability, enabling faster acceleration and more agile handling. Riders could now tackle jumps, turns, and rough terrain with greater precision.

2. The Emergence of Two-Stroke Engines

The introduction of two-stroke engines was a game-changer in motocross history. Lightweight and powerful, these engines provided the torque and acceleration needed for off-road racing. Brands like Suzuki and Yamaha capitalized on this technology, producing models like the Suzuki RM125 and Yamaha YZ250, which dominated tracks in the 1970s and 1980s.

However, the environmental impact and higher maintenance requirements of two-stroke engines eventually led to a resurgence of four-stroke engines in the 1990s. Thanks to advancements in fuel injection and engine design, modern four-stroke engines offer comparable performance with greater efficiency and reliability.

3. Suspension Systems

Suspension technology has arguably been one of the most impactful advancements in motocross. In the early days, bikes had minimal suspension travel, forcing riders to rely on their bodies to absorb impacts. The 1970s saw the advent of long-travel suspension systems, such as Yamaha's Mono-Shock, which significantly improved comfort and control on rough terrain.

Modern suspension systems, featuring adjustable shocks and electronic damping, allow riders to fine-tune their bikes to specific track conditions. These advancements have not only enhanced performance but also reduced fatigue and injury risks for riders.

4. Tire Technology

The development of specialized tires has also played a critical role in motocross. Early tires were not designed for off-road conditions, making traction a constant challenge. Modern motocross tires feature knobby patterns optimized for different terrains, from soft sand to hard-packed dirt. Advances in rubber compounds and tread designs have given riders the grip and durability needed to push their limits.

5. Safety Gear

Safety gear has come a long way since the early days of motocross. Riders initially relied on leather jackets and goggles for protection, offering minimal defense against crashes. The introduction of helmets, body armor, and advanced materials like Kevlar and carbon fiber has significantly reduced injury risks. Modern helmets with MIPS (Multi-directional Impact Protection System) technology and airbag-equipped vests showcase how safety remains a top priority in the sport.

Challenges Riders Faced Before the Digital Era

While technological advancements have transformed motocross, riders in the early days faced numerous challenges that would be unthinkable today. These challenges tested their resilience, ingenuity, and adaptability.

1. Lack of Reliable Equipment

In the sport's infancy, motorcycles were not designed for off-road racing. Riders had to modify street bikes themselves, often using trial and error to adapt their machines for rugged terrain. Breakdowns were common, and riders had to be skilled mechanics to stay in the race.

Even as manufacturers began producing off-road-specific bikes, reliability remained a challenge. Components like engines, suspension systems, and tires were prone to wear and tear, requiring constant maintenance. Riders had to balance the physical demands of racing with the technical knowledge needed to keep their bikes running.

2. Limited Access to Training Resources

Training in the pre-digital era was a matter of intuition and experience. Riders had no access to the data-driven tools and simulations available today. Progress was achieved through sheer practice, often involving countless hours on the track. Without analytics or feedback systems, riders relied on observation and feedback from coaches to improve their skills.

This lack of structured training made it difficult for newcomers to break into the sport. Only those with natural talent and access to experienced mentors could hope to succeed.

3. Navigating Unpredictable Track Conditions

Tracks in the early days of motocross were far from standardized. Riders often faced natural courses with unpredictable terrain, including hidden obstacles and uneven surfaces. Without tools to analyze or map these tracks, riders had to rely on instinct and memory to navigate them.

Weather conditions added another layer of complexity. Rain could turn a track into a slippery mess, while dry conditions created dust clouds that obscured visibility. Riders had to adapt on the fly, often learning the hard way how to handle such challenges.

4. Safety Risks

Motocross has always been a dangerous sport, but the risks were far greater before modern safety advancements. Early riders lacked protective gear, and the bikes themselves were less forgiving. Crashes often resulted in severe injuries, and the medical support available at events was minimal.

Riders also had limited knowledge of how to prevent injuries through proper technique and conditioning. The lack of structured fitness programs meant that many riders were unprepared for the physical toll of the sport.

Looking Ahead

Understanding the history of motocross is essential to appreciating how far the sport has come and where it is headed. From its humble beginnings as a test of endurance to its current status as a global phenomenon, motocross has always been about pushing boundaries.

The challenges faced by early riders laid the foundation for the innovations we see today. As we move into the era of artificial intelligence, motocross is set to undergo another transformation. AI promises to address many of the challenges that have long defined the sport, from optimizing bike performance to enhancing rider safety.

The next section of this chapter will explore the emergence of AI in sports and its potential to revolutionize motocross, offering a glimpse of what lies ahead for riders, teams, and fans.

Section 2: The Emergence of AI in Sports

Artificial intelligence (AI) is one of the most transformative forces in modern society, and its impact on sports is undeniable. From optimizing athlete performance to engaging fans in innovative ways, AI has ushered in a new era for the sports industry. In this section, we will define AI and its capabilities, explore how it is being used in other sports, and examine the potential of AI to revolutionize motocross racing.

Defining AI and Its Capabilities

Artificial intelligence, at its core, refers to the simulation of human intelligence by machines. It enables systems to perform tasks that typically require human cognitive skills, such as learning, reasoning, problem-solving, and decision-making. Through techniques like machine learning (ML), neural networks, and natural language processing, AI systems can analyze vast amounts of data, identify patterns, and make predictions or recommendations.

The power of AI lies in its ability to process and analyze data at speeds and scales that are impossible for humans. Whether it's analyzing player movements in real-time, predicting injury risks, or simulating race strategies, AI provides insights that are both accurate and actionable. Some of its key capabilities include:

1. Data Analysis and Pattern Recognition

AI systems excel at analyzing large datasets to identify patterns and trends. For instance, in sports, AI can analyze performance data to uncover factors that contribute to an athlete's success or failure. In motocross, this could mean analyzing telemetry data from bikes to optimize engine performance or track rider behaviors during races.

2. Predictive Analytics

AI's predictive capabilities are among its most valuable assets. By analyzing historical data, AI can forecast future outcomes with remarkable accuracy. For example, predictive analytics can anticipate weather conditions, competitor performance, or even potential bike failures, enabling riders and teams to prepare in advance.

3. Automation and Efficiency

AI automates repetitive and time-consuming tasks, allowing athletes and teams to focus on what matters most. In motocross, AI can automate tasks like bike diagnostics, race strategy planning, and post-race analysis, freeing up time for riders and engineers to refine their skills and strategies.

4. Real-Time Decision Support

AI systems can provide real-time feedback and recommendations during events. For instance, wearable sensors paired with AI algorithms can monitor a rider's heart rate, positioning, and speed during a race, offering immediate suggestions to improve performance or reduce risks.

Examples of AI in Other Sports: Lessons for Motocross

AI is already transforming a wide range of sports, providing valuable lessons for the motocross community. By examining how AI is being used in other disciplines, we can gain insights into its potential applications in motocross.

1. Soccer: Performance Analytics and Injury Prevention

In soccer, AI is used extensively to monitor player performance and reduce the risk of injuries. Wearable devices track metrics like distance covered, sprint speed, and fatigue levels. This data is analyzed by AI systems to identify signs of overtraining or potential injury risks, allowing teams to adjust training regimens accordingly.

Lesson for Motocross: In motocross, similar wearable technologies could monitor a rider's physical condition during practice and races. This data could help prevent fatigue-related mistakes and injuries, ensuring riders are always in peak condition.

2. Formula 1: Race Strategy and Vehicle Optimization

Formula 1 is one of the most technologically advanced sports in the world, and AI plays a crucial role in its success. Teams use AI-powered simulations to predict race outcomes based on variables like weather, tire choices, and competitor performance. Additionally, AI is used to optimize vehicle aerodynamics and engine performance.

Lesson for Motocross: Like Formula 1 cars, motocross bikes could benefit from AI-driven optimization. By analyzing telemetry data, AI could recommend adjustments to suspension settings, tire pressure, or engine tuning, ensuring bikes are perfectly calibrated for specific track conditions.

3. Tennis: Shot Analysis and Coaching

AI-powered tools like IBM's Watson have revolutionized tennis coaching by analyzing match footage and player movements. These systems provide insights into shot selection, court positioning, and opponent tendencies, enabling players to refine their strategies.

Lesson for Motocross: In motocross, AI could analyze video footage of a rider's performance to identify areas for improvement, such as cornering techniques, jump landings, or throttle control. This feedback could be invaluable for both amateur and professional riders.

4. Baseball: Fan Engagement and Content Creation

AI is also transforming the way fans interact with sports. In baseball, AI is used to generate highlights, analyze player statistics, and create personalized content for fans. These innovations enhance the spectator experience and drive engagement.

Lesson for Motocross: Motocross could use AI to create dynamic content for fans, such as real-time race analytics, personalized highlights, and virtual track simulations. This could make the sport more accessible and engaging for a broader audience.

The Potential of AI to Transform Motocross Racing

Motocross, with its unique combination of physical skill, mechanical precision, and environmental challenges, stands to benefit immensely from AI. Here are some of the key areas where AI could revolutionize the sport:

1. Personalized Rider Training

AI-powered training systems could provide motocross riders with highly personalized feedback and recommendations. By analyzing data from wearable sensors, video footage, and telemetry systems, AI could create custom training plans tailored to each rider's strengths and weaknesses.

For example, an AI system could identify that a rider consistently loses time on certain types of corners. By analyzing their body positioning, braking patterns, and throttle control, the system could provide actionable advice to help them improve. Over time, this personalized approach could accelerate skill development and enhance performance.

2. Advanced Bike Maintenance

Motocross bikes endure extreme wear and tear, making maintenance a critical aspect of the sport. AI-powered diagnostic systems could revolutionize how bikes are maintained by predicting potential issues before they occur.

For instance, AI could analyze data from sensors embedded in the bike to detect subtle changes in engine performance, suspension behavior, or tire wear. This predictive capability would allow teams to address issues proactively, reducing the risk of mechanical failures during races.

3. Real-Time Race Strategy

During a race, split-second decisions can make the difference between victory and defeat. AI systems could provide real-time recommendations to riders based on track conditions, competitor positions, and performance metrics.

For example, an AI tool could suggest the fastest lines through a particular section of the track or recommend when to push for overtaking opportunities. These insights could give riders a strategic edge, helping them stay ahead of the competition.

4. Enhanced Safety Measures

Safety is a top priority in motocross, and AI could play a pivotal role in reducing risks. Wearable devices paired with AI algorithms could monitor a rider's vital signs, fatigue levels, and crash risks during races. If the system detects signs of danger, it could alert the rider or team in real time.

Additionally, AI-powered simulations could help riders prepare for challenging track conditions, reducing the likelihood of accidents. By simulating various scenarios, riders could develop the skills and confidence needed to handle even the toughest challenges.

5. Fan Engagement and Growth

AI could also help motocross reach new audiences by enhancing the spectator experience. AI-powered platforms could provide fans with real-time analytics, personalized content, and interactive features. For example, fans could use virtual reality (VR) simulations to experience tracks from a rider's perspective or analyze races using AI-generated insights.

By making motocross more engaging and accessible, these innovations could attract new fans and drive the sport's growth.

Looking Ahead

The emergence of AI in sports marks a new chapter in the evolution of motocross. By learning from other sports and embracing the potential of AI, motocross riders, teams, and fans can unlock unprecedented opportunities for growth and innovation.

As we continue to explore the intersection of AI and motocross in this book, we'll delve deeper into how these technologies can be applied in practical, impactful ways. From training and strategy to bike maintenance and fan engagement, the possibilities are endless.

Motocross has always been about pushing boundaries—of speed, skill, and courage. With AI, the sport is poised to push those boundaries even further, redefining what's possible on the dirt track.

Section 3: Why AI Matters in Motocross

Motocross is one of the most demanding motorsports in the world, requiring not only exceptional physical and mental endurance from riders but also precise bike performance and adaptability to ever-changing track conditions. These unique demands create challenges that traditional tools and methods struggle to address. However, artificial intelligence (AI) offers innovative solutions that can revolutionize how motocross is approached, from training and bike optimization to track design and safety. In this section, we'll examine the unique demands of motocross racing, explore how AI addresses key challenges, and discuss the future synergy between AI and motocross.

The Unique Demands of Motocross Racing

Motocross is unlike any other motorsport, combining the raw power of off-road motorcycles with the unpredictable dynamics of dirt tracks. Riders face a variety of challenges that test their skill, endurance, and decision-making abilities in ways that other sports do not.

1. Physical and Mental Demands on Riders

Motocross riders are athletes in every sense of the word. The sport requires immense physical strength, particularly in the core, arms, and legs, to control the bike and maintain balance over rough terrain. Races often last 30 minutes or longer, during which riders must constantly adjust their position, throttle, and braking to navigate obstacles like jumps, berms, and ruts.

The mental demands are equally intense. Riders must process information rapidly, from evaluating track conditions and competitor positions to adjusting their strategies on the fly.

Fatigue can compromise reaction times and decision-making, increasing the risk of mistakes and accidents.

2. The Complexity of Bike Performance

Motocross bikes are high-performance machines designed to handle extreme conditions, but their complexity poses challenges for riders and mechanics alike. Suspension settings, tire pressure, engine tuning, and gear ratios all need to be optimized for specific track conditions. A small error in setup can significantly impact performance, making it difficult for riders to compete at their best.

Unlike other motorsports with paved tracks, motocross bikes face constant wear and tear from dirt, mud, and debris. Maintenance is a constant battle, with teams needing to monitor and address issues like overheating, chain wear, and suspension fatigue.

3. The Ever-Changing Nature of Tracks

Motocross tracks are dynamic environments. Unlike the fixed asphalt circuits of road racing, dirt tracks evolve throughout a race. Jumps, berms, and ruts change shape as riders pass over them, altering the optimal racing line. Weather conditions, such as rain or heat, further complicate matters by affecting traction and visibility.

For riders and teams, predicting how a track will evolve is a significant challenge. A strategy that works in the early laps may become ineffective as the track deteriorates, requiring constant adaptation.

How AI Addresses Rider, Bike, and Track Challenges

The unique demands of motocross make it an ideal candidate for the transformative power of AI. By leveraging AI's ability to analyze data, predict outcomes, and optimize performance, riders and teams can gain a competitive edge while improving safety and efficiency.

1. Enhancing Rider Performance

AI can play a pivotal role in helping riders reach their full potential by providing insights and recommendations tailored to their individual needs.

a. Wearable Sensors for Real-Time Monitoring
Wearable devices equipped with sensors can monitor a rider's physical condition, including heart rate, hydration levels, and muscle fatigue. AI algorithms analyze this data in real time, providing feedback to help riders manage their energy levels and avoid overexertion.

b. Skill Development Through Video Analysis
AI-powered video analysis tools can review footage of training sessions and races, identifying areas where a rider can improve. For example, the system might highlight

inefficiencies in cornering technique or suboptimal body positioning during jumps, providing actionable advice to enhance performance.

c. Mental Preparation and Focus

AI can also assist riders in developing mental resilience. By analyzing patterns in their performance data, AI systems can identify factors that lead to lapses in focus or poor decision-making. Riders can use this information to refine their mental strategies, improving concentration and reaction times under pressure.

2. Optimizing Bike Performance

Motocross bikes are highly sensitive to setup adjustments, and AI offers unprecedented precision in optimizing their performance.

a. Predictive Maintenance

AI-powered diagnostic tools can monitor the health of key bike components, such as the engine, suspension, and chain. By detecting subtle signs of wear and predicting potential failures, these systems enable teams to perform maintenance proactively, reducing the risk of breakdowns during races.

b. Dynamic Tuning for Track Conditions

AI systems can analyze track data and recommend adjustments to suspension settings, tire pressure, and gear ratios based on current conditions. For example, if a track becomes muddy due to rain, the AI might suggest softer suspension and lower tire pressure to improve traction.

c. Performance Data Integration

Modern motocross bikes are often equipped with telemetry systems that collect data on factors like throttle input, braking force, and lean angle. AI can process this data to identify areas where the bike's performance can be improved, ensuring that every component is working in harmony.

3. Tackling Track Challenges

AI's ability to analyze and predict environmental variables makes it a powerful tool for navigating the complexities of motocross tracks.

a. Track Evolution Prediction

AI algorithms can analyze track data, including soil composition, moisture levels, and rider behavior, to predict how the track will change over the course of a race. This information allows riders to anticipate evolving conditions and adjust their strategies accordingly.

b. Virtual Track Simulations

Before a race, riders and teams can use AI-powered simulations to practice on virtual versions of the track. These simulations incorporate factors like elevation changes, jump heights, and weather conditions, providing a realistic training environment that helps riders develop their strategies.

c. Safety Enhancements

AI can also improve track safety by identifying high-risk areas prone to accidents, such as sharp turns or blind jumps. Event organizers can use this information to make targeted improvements, reducing the likelihood of crashes.

The Future of AI and Motocross Synergy

The integration of AI into motocross is still in its early stages, but the possibilities are limitless. As AI technology continues to advance, its impact on the sport is expected to grow, transforming every aspect of motocross from training and bike design to fan engagement and sustainability.

1. Autonomous Testing and Development

In the future, AI could enable autonomous testing of motocross bikes, allowing manufacturers to simulate thousands of race scenarios without human riders. These simulations could accelerate the development of new technologies, such as lightweight materials and advanced suspension systems, pushing the boundaries of bike performance.

2. AI-Driven Coaching Platforms

AI-powered coaching platforms could provide riders with personalized training programs based on their unique strengths and weaknesses. These platforms would integrate data from wearable sensors, video footage, and telemetry systems, creating a comprehensive picture of each rider's performance.

3. Sustainability and Environmental Impact

As motocross faces growing pressure to reduce its environmental impact, AI could play a key role in promoting sustainability. For example, AI systems could optimize fuel consumption and emissions in motocross bikes, making them more eco-friendly. Additionally, AI could help design tracks that minimize environmental disruption while maintaining the thrill of the sport.

4. Enhancing Fan Engagement

AI has the potential to revolutionize how fans experience motocross. Real-time analytics, virtual reality simulations, and interactive content could make the sport more engaging and accessible to a global audience. Fans could use AI-powered apps to track their favorite riders, analyze race data, and even participate in virtual races.

5. Collaboration Between Humans and AI

Ultimately, the future of motocross will be defined by collaboration between humans and AI. While AI provides valuable insights and tools, the creativity, intuition, and passion of riders and teams will remain at the heart of the sport. Together, humans and AI can push the limits of what's possible, taking motocross to new heights.

Looking Ahead

The unique demands of motocross make it a challenging yet rewarding sport, and AI offers transformative solutions to its most pressing challenges. By enhancing rider performance, optimizing bike setups, and addressing track complexities, AI has the potential to revolutionize motocross in ways we are only beginning to imagine.

As we explore the future of motocross in this book, it becomes clear that the synergy between AI and motocross is not just a possibility—it's an inevitability. The riders, teams, and organizations that embrace AI will lead the charge into a new era of competition, innovation, and excitement.

Chapter 2: AI-Powered Training for Riders

Section 1: Personalized Training Programs

In the high-stakes world of motocross, where milliseconds can mean the difference between victory and defeat, personalized training is critical. Traditional training methods often rely on generalized programs that may not address the unique needs of individual riders. However, the integration of artificial intelligence (AI) has revolutionized how training programs are designed and executed. With wearable technology, AI-driven recommendations, and adaptive training plans, riders can now optimize their physical and mental preparation to achieve peak performance.

The Role of Wearables in Collecting Data

Wearable technology has become a cornerstone of modern training programs, offering unprecedented insights into a rider's physical and physiological performance. These devices, ranging from smartwatches to advanced biometric sensors, collect data in real time, enabling riders and coaches to make informed decisions about their training routines.

1. Types of Wearable Devices Used in Motocross

Motocross riders use various types of wearable devices to monitor key performance metrics. These include:

- **Heart Rate Monitors**: Track heart rate variability to gauge cardiovascular health and recovery.
- **GPS Trackers**: Measure speed, distance, and positioning on the track.
- **Motion Sensors**: Analyze body movements, including lean angles and jumping techniques.
- **Muscle Activity Sensors**: Detect muscle engagement and fatigue during rides.

These devices work together to provide a comprehensive view of a rider's performance, creating a foundation for data-driven training programs.

2. Real-Time Data Collection and Feedback

Wearable technology collects data continuously during training sessions and races. This real-time feedback allows riders to identify areas for improvement immediately. For example, a rider struggling with cornering technique might notice excessive muscle tension or poor balance through wearable data, prompting adjustments in their approach.

AI plays a crucial role by processing this data and presenting it in an easily understandable format. Complex metrics are translated into actionable insights, such as recommending specific stretches to alleviate muscle strain or suggesting modifications to body posture.

3. Monitoring Recovery and Preventing Injuries

Recovery is just as important as training in motocross, given the sport's physically demanding nature. Wearables equipped with AI algorithms can monitor recovery metrics like heart rate variability, sleep patterns, and hydration levels.

By identifying early signs of fatigue or overtraining, these devices help riders avoid injuries that could sideline them for weeks or months. For instance, if a rider's wearable detects a decrease in recovery metrics, their training program can be adjusted to include more rest days or lighter workouts.

AI-Driven Fitness and Endurance Recommendations

Fitness and endurance are critical for motocross riders, who must maintain control of their bikes under intense physical and mental stress. AI takes the guesswork out of fitness training by providing tailored recommendations based on a rider's unique physiology, performance data, and goals.

1. Customizing Workouts Based on Data

AI systems analyze data from wearables and other sources to design personalized workout plans. These plans take into account factors such as:

- **Current Fitness Levels**: Determined by metrics like VO2 max, resting heart rate, and muscle endurance.
- **Training Objectives**: Whether the rider aims to improve speed, stamina, or overall strength.
- **Physiological Responses**: How the rider's body reacts to different types of exercise.

For example, a rider looking to enhance endurance might receive a plan focused on long-duration cardio sessions and interval training. Meanwhile, a rider aiming to improve strength might focus on resistance training and plyometric exercises.

2. Nutrition and Hydration Guidance

AI doesn't stop at workout plans; it also provides guidance on nutrition and hydration, which are vital for peak performance. By analyzing data on caloric expenditure, sweat composition, and hydration levels, AI can recommend:

- **Pre-Race Meals**: Optimized for energy and focus.
- **Post-Workout Recovery Nutrition**: Including protein and carbohydrate ratios for muscle repair.
- **Hydration Strategies**: Adjusted for weather conditions and individual sweat rates.

For instance, a rider training in hot weather might receive AI-generated advice to increase electrolyte intake to prevent dehydration.

3. Tracking and Enhancing Endurance

Motocross requires sustained physical effort, often under extreme conditions. AI systems help riders build endurance by tracking performance over time and identifying areas for improvement.

- **Progressive Overload**: AI can adjust training intensity gradually, ensuring that riders build stamina without risking overtraining.
- **Interval Training Optimization**: By analyzing heart rate and oxygen consumption data, AI can create interval workouts tailored to a rider's specific aerobic and anaerobic thresholds.
- **Recovery Metrics**: AI ensures that riders have adequate rest between sessions to maximize endurance gains.

Adapting Training Plans Based on Progress

One of AI's most powerful capabilities is its ability to adapt training programs dynamically based on a rider's progress. Unlike static training plans, AI-driven programs evolve in response to real-world data, ensuring continuous improvement and preventing plateaus.

1. Continuous Performance Analysis

AI systems continuously analyze performance metrics to assess a rider's progress. This includes evaluating factors like:

- **Improvements in Speed and Agility**: Measured through GPS and motion sensors.
- **Physical Adaptations**: Such as increased strength or endurance, detected through biometric data.
- **Technique Refinements**: Identified through video analysis and motion tracking.

If progress slows or stalls, the AI can identify the root cause—whether it's inadequate recovery, poor technique, or a mismatch between training intensity and goals—and recommend adjustments.

2. Dynamic Goal Setting

As riders achieve their initial training objectives, AI systems help them set new, more challenging goals. This dynamic goal-setting process ensures that training remains engaging and effective.

For example, a rider who successfully improves their lap times on a specific track might be encouraged to tackle more complex courses or focus on advanced techniques like scrubbing or whip jumps.

3. Adapting to External Factors

Motocross training doesn't happen in a vacuum; external factors like weather, track conditions, and competition schedules play a significant role. AI systems can adapt training plans to account for these variables.

- **Weather-Responsive Training**: If rain is forecasted, the AI might suggest practicing on muddy tracks to prepare for similar race conditions.
- **Event Preparation**: AI can adjust the intensity and focus of training in the weeks leading up to a major competition, ensuring that riders peak at the right time.

By integrating external factors into training plans, AI helps riders stay prepared for any situation they might encounter on race day.

Conclusion

The integration of AI into motocross training has transformed how riders prepare for the challenges of the sport. Wearable technology collects invaluable data on physical performance, AI-driven systems provide personalized fitness and endurance recommendations, and adaptive training plans ensure continuous progress. Together, these innovations empower riders to push their limits while minimizing the risks of overtraining and injury.

As motocross continues to evolve, the role of AI in training will only grow more significant. Riders who embrace these technologies will gain a competitive edge, achieving levels of performance that were once thought impossible. By leveraging the power of AI, the next generation of motocross athletes will redefine what it means to dominate the track.

Section 2: Skill Development Through AI

Mastering the technical and tactical aspects of motocross riding requires dedication, precision, and an understanding of how to adapt to constantly changing conditions. Traditional training methods, while effective to an extent, are often limited by subjective observations and static routines. Artificial intelligence (AI) is revolutionizing this space by offering innovative tools to analyze riding techniques, simulate race environments, and provide real-time feedback for improvement. In this section, we'll explore how AI can enhance skill development by analyzing riding techniques through machine learning, using simulation tools to practice in virtual environments, and leveraging feedback mechanisms for instant improvements.

Analyzing Riding Techniques Using Machine Learning

AI, powered by machine learning algorithms, is transforming how motocross riders assess and refine their techniques. These systems analyze vast amounts of data from training sessions, identifying patterns and offering targeted insights that were previously unavailable.

1. Capturing and Analyzing Rider Data

Machine learning systems use data collected from sensors, cameras, and telemetry systems to evaluate a rider's performance. The captured data includes:

- **Body Position**: Lean angles, posture during jumps, and transitions between positions.
- **Throttle and Brake Usage**: Patterns of acceleration, deceleration, and cornering techniques.
- **Line Selection**: The paths riders take through the track and their efficiency.

For example, motion sensors on the bike and the rider's gear can track body movements during a lap. By comparing these movements against those of top-performing riders, AI systems identify inefficiencies or areas for improvement.

2. Identifying Patterns and Weaknesses

Machine learning excels at recognizing subtle patterns that may not be apparent to even the most experienced coaches. For instance, an AI system might detect that a rider consistently loses time in left-hand corners due to improper weight distribution.

By analyzing repeated actions and outcomes, machine learning models can pinpoint weaknesses, such as:

- Over-braking in certain track sections.
- Inconsistent throttle application during jumps.
- Poor body positioning in rough terrain.

With this information, riders can focus their practice on addressing specific weaknesses, making their training more efficient and goal-oriented.

3. Building Personalized Riding Profiles

AI systems also create personalized riding profiles that serve as benchmarks for improvement. These profiles track metrics like lap times, cornering speeds, and jump heights over time, allowing riders to see how their skills evolve.

The profiles can be shared with coaches, enabling data-driven discussions about technique refinement. For example, a coach might use the profile to demonstrate how changes in body position improved lap times by reducing drag or enhancing stability.

Simulation Tools for Practicing in a Virtual Environment

Virtual simulation tools are becoming increasingly popular in motocross training, offering riders a safe and controlled environment to practice and experiment. Powered by AI, these tools replicate real-world tracks and conditions with astonishing accuracy, providing riders with a unique opportunity to refine their skills.

1. Creating Realistic Track Simulations

AI-driven simulation tools use detailed data about track layouts, soil composition, and weather conditions to create virtual environments that mirror actual race tracks. These simulations include:

- **Dynamic Track Changes**: Simulating how the track evolves during a race, such as ruts deepening and berms breaking down.
- **Environmental Factors**: Incorporating variables like rain, wind, and temperature to mimic real-world challenges.
- **Competitor Behavior**: AI can simulate the actions of other riders, creating scenarios that test decision-making skills.

For instance, a rider preparing for a specific event can practice on a virtual replica of the track, learning the fastest lines and anticipating how conditions might change during the race.

2. Practicing High-Risk Maneuvers Safely

One of the greatest advantages of simulation tools is the ability to practice high-risk maneuvers without the danger of physical injury. Riders can experiment with techniques like scrubbing, whip jumps, and aggressive cornering in a virtual environment, building confidence and skill before applying them on the track.

By analyzing the outcomes of these virtual sessions, AI systems provide feedback on what works and what doesn't. For example, the AI might suggest adjustments to the timing of a scrub maneuver to maximize speed over jumps.

3. Enhancing Mental Preparation

Simulations aren't just about physical skills; they also help riders prepare mentally. Virtual environments allow riders to:

- **Visualize Races**: Experience the track layout and key sections before the event.
- **Practice Decision-Making**: Respond to simulated scenarios, such as navigating through traffic or recovering from a mistake.
- **Build Race-Day Confidence**: Familiarity with the track and conditions reduces pre-race anxiety.

Overall, simulation tools create a comprehensive training experience that combines physical skill-building with mental preparation.

Feedback Mechanisms for Real-Time Improvement

AI-powered feedback mechanisms enable riders to receive instant, actionable insights during training sessions. These systems bridge the gap between practice and performance, helping riders make adjustments in real time to achieve better results.

1. Live Performance Monitoring

Wearable devices and telemetry systems provide continuous feedback on key performance metrics during training. AI systems process this data in real time, offering insights such as:

- **Optimal Throttle Control**: Suggestions for smoother acceleration and deceleration.
- **Improved Cornering Technique**: Feedback on body positioning and lean angles.
- **Jump Timing and Execution**: Guidance on takeoff and landing techniques.

For example, a rider practicing on a rough track might receive immediate feedback about their body posture, helping them adjust to maintain stability and control.

2. Audio and Visual Cues

AI systems can deliver feedback through audio or visual cues, ensuring that riders stay focused on their performance. Examples include:

- **Audible Alerts**: A beep or voice prompt indicating when to adjust throttle or braking.
- **On-Screen Displays**: Real-time metrics displayed on a helmet visor or handlebar-mounted screen.

These cues allow riders to make corrections without interrupting their flow, maximizing the effectiveness of each training session.

3. Post-Session Analysis for Long-Term Gains

After a training session, AI systems provide detailed analyses of performance, highlighting areas for improvement and tracking progress over time. These post-session reports often include:

- **Heat Maps**: Visual representations of track sections where the rider excelled or struggled.
- **Comparative Data**: Side-by-side comparisons of different laps to identify trends.
- **Actionable Recommendations**: Specific drills or exercises to address weaknesses.

By reviewing these analyses, riders and coaches can develop targeted training plans that address specific challenges, ensuring continuous improvement.

Skill development in motocross has always been a challenging and iterative process, requiring riders to balance physical endurance, technical precision, and mental focus. AI has introduced a new era of training, offering tools and insights that were previously unimaginable.

Machine learning enables riders to analyze their techniques with unparalleled depth, identifying subtle patterns and inefficiencies that hinder performance. Virtual simulation tools provide a safe and dynamic environment for practicing high-risk maneuvers and building race-day confidence. Real-time feedback mechanisms ensure that riders can make immediate adjustments during training, bridging the gap between practice and performance.

As motocross continues to evolve, the integration of AI into training programs will become increasingly essential. Riders who embrace these technologies will not only enhance their skills but also gain a competitive edge in a sport where every detail matters. The synergy between human skill and AI innovation promises to unlock new levels of performance, transforming motocross into a sport where the boundaries of possibility are constantly being redefined.

Section 3: Mental Preparation Using AI Tools

In the high-pressure environment of motocross, mental preparation is as vital as physical training. Riders face intense demands, from maintaining focus during high-speed maneuvers to overcoming the psychological toll of competition. Traditionally, mental resilience and stress management relied on experience and human coaching, but the integration of artificial intelligence (AI) has introduced groundbreaking tools to enhance mental preparedness. This section explores how AI builds mental resilience, incorporates gamification techniques for training motivation, and uses predictive models to manage stress and fatigue effectively.

Using AI to Build Mental Resilience

Mental resilience is the ability to remain focused, composed, and adaptive under pressure—qualities that are indispensable in motocross. AI technologies now play a critical role in helping riders develop these traits by providing data-driven insights and personalized strategies.

1. Cognitive Training with AI-Driven Programs

AI-powered platforms can improve cognitive functions like focus, reaction time, and decision-making. These programs analyze a rider's cognitive performance over time and provide tailored exercises to strengthen mental faculties.

For example, apps like **NeuroTracker** or similar AI-driven tools assess and enhance a rider's:

- **Situational Awareness**: Simulating fast-paced scenarios to help riders process visual and spatial information more quickly.
- **Reaction Times**: Training to anticipate and respond to obstacles or track changes.
- **Decision-Making Under Pressure**: Exercises designed to simulate race-day stress and encourage quick, effective choices.

By regularly engaging with these programs, riders can enhance their mental agility, enabling them to stay sharp even in high-pressure situations.

2. Virtual Reality (VR) for Mental Conditioning

AI-integrated VR systems provide a realistic and immersive environment where riders can simulate race conditions. This approach helps riders acclimate to the pressure of competition without the physical risks associated with on-track practice.

For instance, riders can:

- Practice visualizing their performance on specific tracks.
- Train to remain calm while navigating virtual scenarios involving crashes or aggressive competitors.
- Develop coping mechanisms for unexpected events, such as poor starts or mechanical issues.

By repeatedly experiencing these simulated scenarios, riders can build confidence and mental resilience for real-world races.

3. Monitoring and Improving Emotional Regulation

AI-enabled biometric devices, such as heart rate monitors and EEG headsets, track stress indicators during training or simulation sessions. These tools help riders:

- Recognize their emotional triggers, such as anxiety before a difficult section of a track.
- Implement strategies like mindfulness exercises or breathing techniques, guided by AI-generated suggestions.

For example, if a rider's heart rate spikes during practice, the AI might recommend a brief meditation session or calming exercises to regain focus. Over time, these interventions help riders build emotional control and maintain composure during races.

Gamification Techniques for Training Motivation

Motocross training can be grueling, and maintaining motivation over long periods is a common challenge. Gamification—the application of game-like elements to training—has emerged as a powerful tool to make training engaging and enjoyable. AI enhances this process by creating personalized, adaptive challenges that keep riders motivated.

1. Turning Training into a Rewarding Experience

AI-powered platforms can gamify training sessions by incorporating:

- **Point Systems**: Rewarding riders for completing specific tasks, such as improving lap times or mastering a technique.
- **Leaderboards**: Allowing riders to compete with peers or their past performances.
- **Achievements**: Unlocking badges or rewards for milestones, like completing a flawless virtual lap.

For example, an AI system might challenge a rider to achieve a 5% improvement in their cornering speed over a week. Each day, the rider receives feedback and incremental rewards, fostering a sense of accomplishment.

2. Adaptive Challenges for Continuous Engagement

AI-driven gamification adapts to a rider's skill level and progress, ensuring that challenges remain stimulating but not overwhelming. For instance:

- If a rider excels in straight-line speed but struggles with jumps, the AI might create mini-games focused on jump timing and execution.
- As the rider improves, the AI gradually increases the difficulty, maintaining a balance between challenge and competence.

This dynamic approach prevents monotony and keeps riders engaged throughout their training journey.

3. Social and Collaborative Elements

AI platforms can introduce social elements to training, fostering a sense of community and friendly competition. Riders can:

- Share their scores or achievements with teammates.
- Participate in virtual races against AI-simulated competitors or other riders.
- Collaborate on team challenges, such as collectively reducing lap times on a specific track.

These features not only boost motivation but also encourage riders to learn from each other, accelerating their development.

Predictive Models for Stress and Fatigue Management

Motocross is a physically and mentally demanding sport, and stress or fatigue can significantly impact performance. AI's predictive capabilities are transforming how riders monitor and manage these factors, ensuring they remain at their best.

1. Predicting Stress Levels with Biometric Data

AI systems analyze biometric data collected from wearables to predict stress levels and provide timely interventions. Key metrics include:

- **Heart Rate Variability (HRV)**: Low HRV often indicates heightened stress or inadequate recovery.
- **Cortisol Levels**: Measured indirectly through skin sensors or other biomarkers.
- **Sleep Quality**: Monitored through devices like smartwatches to detect restlessness or interruptions.

For example, if an AI detects that a rider's HRV has been consistently low for several days, it might recommend lighter training sessions or mindfulness exercises to reduce stress.

2. Managing Fatigue Through Training Adjustments

Fatigue is a major risk factor in motocross, leading to poor performance and increased injury risk. AI systems use predictive models to monitor a rider's workload and recovery, ensuring optimal performance.

- **Tracking Workload Metrics**: AI calculates cumulative training stress by analyzing metrics like session duration, intensity, and frequency.
- **Recommending Rest Periods**: Based on fatigue indicators, the AI adjusts training plans to include adequate rest and recovery days.
- **Identifying Overtraining Risks**: By comparing current performance metrics with historical data, AI can flag early signs of overtraining, allowing riders to address the issue proactively.

3. Enhancing Long-Term Recovery and Performance

AI's predictive capabilities extend beyond short-term fatigue management to long-term performance optimization. Riders benefit from:

- **Periodized Training Plans**: AI designs programs that alternate between high-intensity and recovery phases to maximize performance gains.
- **Seasonal Insights**: Predicting how stress and fatigue levels fluctuate throughout the racing season, helping riders plan their training and rest accordingly.
- **Mental Fatigue Monitoring**: Identifying signs of burnout, such as decreased motivation or focus, and recommending interventions like mental health check-ins or relaxation techniques.

For instance, an AI system might detect that a rider is more prone to mental fatigue after consecutive high-pressure events. In response, it could suggest incorporating mindfulness exercises or reducing cognitive load during training sessions.

Mental preparation is a cornerstone of success in motocross, and AI tools are reshaping how riders build resilience, stay motivated, and manage stress. By leveraging cognitive training programs, immersive simulations, and real-time biometric feedback, AI enables riders to enhance their mental toughness and perform under pressure. Gamification adds an element of fun and engagement to training, while predictive models ensure that stress and fatigue are managed effectively, safeguarding both short-term performance and long-term well-being.

As the synergy between AI and motocross continues to evolve, mental preparation will become increasingly data-driven and personalized. Riders who embrace these advancements will not only sharpen their mental edge but also unlock new levels of performance, ensuring they stay competitive in a demanding and ever-changing sport. The future of motocross training lies in the seamless integration of AI technologies, where physical and mental preparation are optimized like never before.

Chapter 3: Optimizing Bike Performance with AI

Section 1: AI-Driven Diagnostics

The introduction of AI-driven diagnostics has revolutionized how motocross riders and their teams monitor, maintain, and optimize bike performance. In a sport where split-second decisions and precision engineering determine success, leveraging AI to analyze and predict mechanical performance is a game-changer. This section delves into how sensors monitor bike health, AI identifies potential mechanical issues before they become critical, and preventative maintenance ensures optimal bike performance and longevity.

Using Sensors to Monitor Bike Health

Modern motocross bikes are increasingly equipped with an array of sensors that provide real-time data on various aspects of the bike's performance. AI analyzes this data to ensure that every component operates at peak efficiency.

1. Types of Sensors in Motocross Bikes

Sensors are the foundation of AI-driven diagnostics, collecting data that AI processes to generate actionable insights. Commonly used sensors in motocross include:

- **Engine Sensors**: Monitor parameters like temperature, RPM, and oil pressure to ensure smooth operation.
- **Suspension Sensors**: Track the performance of the suspension system, including compression and rebound rates, helping riders adjust for different track conditions.
- **Brake Sensors**: Measure braking force and pad wear to optimize stopping power.
- **Tire Pressure Sensors**: Ensure consistent traction and minimize the risk of blowouts.

These sensors constantly feed data to the bike's onboard computer or a connected device, providing a comprehensive picture of the bike's health.

2. Real-Time Monitoring for Immediate Feedback

One of the greatest advantages of sensor-based systems is their ability to provide real-time feedback. During a race or training session, riders and teams can receive updates on:

- **Engine Performance**: Early signs of overheating or unusual vibrations.
- **Suspension Adjustments**: Suggestions for optimizing handling based on track conditions.

- **Tire Wear and Pressure**: Alerts when adjustments are needed to maintain grip and stability.

For instance, if a sensor detects that engine oil temperature is rising beyond optimal levels, the AI system can immediately alert the rider to take precautionary measures, such as reducing speed or heading to the pit for inspection.

3. The Role of IoT in Connected Bikes

The Internet of Things (IoT) enables motocross bikes to connect seamlessly with AI platforms. By integrating sensors, cloud computing, and AI, IoT-connected bikes allow for:

- **Remote Monitoring**: Teams can access performance data from anywhere, enabling real-time diagnostics during races.
- **Data Sharing**: Historical data can be shared with engineers and AI systems for in-depth analysis.
- **Continuous Updates**: AI algorithms can improve over time, refining diagnostics and recommendations as more data is collected.

This interconnected approach ensures that every aspect of the bike's performance is meticulously monitored and optimized.

Identifying Mechanical Issues Before They Occur

One of AI's most powerful capabilities is its ability to identify potential mechanical problems before they escalate, minimizing downtime and preventing costly repairs.

1. Predictive Maintenance with Machine Learning

Machine learning algorithms analyze historical data and real-time inputs to predict when and where mechanical failures are likely to occur. Key benefits include:

- **Failure Pattern Recognition**: AI detects patterns in sensor data that indicate wear and tear, such as abnormal vibrations or temperature fluctuations.
- **Anomaly Detection**: By comparing current data to established benchmarks, AI identifies deviations that signal potential issues.

For example, if AI detects a gradual increase in engine vibration over several races, it can alert the team to inspect the engine for possible issues like a misaligned crankshaft or worn-out bearings.

2. Early Detection of Wear and Tear

AI-driven diagnostics can identify wear and tear on critical components long before they fail, allowing for timely intervention. Common areas monitored include:

- **Chain and Sprockets**: AI analyzes power output and chain tension to determine when replacements are needed.

- **Brakes and Rotors**: Sensors measure pad thickness and rotor condition, alerting riders when braking efficiency is compromised.
- **Suspension Components**: AI evaluates data from suspension sensors to detect signs of wear in shocks and seals.

By addressing these issues proactively, riders can avoid breakdowns and maintain consistent performance on the track.

3. Case Study: AI Success in Predicting Failures

The impact of AI-driven diagnostics is evident in real-world applications. For instance:

- **Factory Teams**: Leading motocross teams have adopted AI systems that predict component failures with remarkable accuracy, reducing race-day mishaps.
- **Amateur Riders**: Affordable AI tools now enable even amateur riders to benefit from predictive maintenance, leveling the playing field.

These advancements demonstrate how AI is transforming motocross into a sport where precision and preparation reign supreme.

Preventative Maintenance Recommendations

Preventative maintenance is essential in motocross, where even minor mechanical issues can have significant consequences. AI-driven systems take preventative care to the next level by offering tailored recommendations based on data analysis.

1. Creating Custom Maintenance Schedules

AI systems generate maintenance schedules that are customized to each rider's unique needs. Factors considered include:

- **Riding Style**: Aggressive riders may require more frequent maintenance of components like brakes and suspension.
- **Track Conditions**: Sandy or muddy tracks can accelerate wear and tear, necessitating more frequent checks.
- **Usage Patterns**: Data on ride frequency and intensity helps determine optimal maintenance intervals.

For example, an AI system might recommend inspecting the air filter more frequently for riders who regularly train on dusty tracks.

2. Optimizing Spare Part Inventory

AI helps teams manage spare part inventories efficiently, ensuring they have the right components on hand without overstocking. Benefits include:

- **Demand Forecasting**: Predicting which parts are likely to need replacement based on usage data.

- **Minimizing Downtime**: Ensuring that critical components are always available for quick repairs.

For instance, if AI predicts that a rider's clutch plates are nearing the end of their lifespan, the team can pre-order replacements to avoid delays.

3. Enhancing Longevity Through Data-Driven Insights

AI not only helps prevent breakdowns but also extends the overall lifespan of bike components. Strategies include:

- **Lubrication Monitoring**: Ensuring that engines and chains are adequately lubricated to reduce friction and wear.
- **Load Distribution Analysis**: Adjusting suspension and tire pressure to evenly distribute forces, minimizing stress on components.
- **Heat Management**: Monitoring engine and brake temperatures to prevent overheating and thermal damage.

By following AI-driven recommendations, riders can maximize the performance and durability of their bikes, reducing costs and improving competitiveness.

AI-driven diagnostics represent a paradigm shift in how motocross riders and teams approach bike maintenance. By leveraging sensors to monitor bike health, identifying mechanical issues before they occur, and providing preventative maintenance recommendations, AI ensures that every aspect of a bike's performance is optimized.

These advancements empower riders to focus on their skills and strategy, confident that their equipment is operating at peak efficiency. As AI continues to evolve, the synergy between technology and motocross will only deepen, pushing the boundaries of what is possible on the track.

Section 3: Customizing Bikes for Peak Performance

Motocross racing demands precision-tuned machines capable of handling dynamic terrains, aggressive maneuvers, and ever-changing conditions. Achieving peak performance requires a deep understanding of the bike's mechanics, as well as the unique demands of each race. With the advent of AI, customizing bikes has reached unprecedented levels of precision and efficiency. This section explores how AI tools optimize suspension and tires, adapt engine settings based on terrain data, and make predictive adjustments for weather and track conditions.

AI Tools for Optimizing Suspension and Tires

Properly optimized suspension and tire performance are essential for maintaining control, minimizing fatigue, and maximizing speed on a motocross track. AI tools now play a crucial role in fine-tuning these components to meet the unique demands of every rider and race.

1. Fine-Tuning Suspension with AI Analysis

Suspension setup is critical in motocross, as it directly affects a rider's ability to navigate jumps, corners, and rough terrain. AI systems use data collected from sensors to analyze suspension performance and recommend adjustments.

Key aspects of AI-powered suspension optimization include:

- **Compression and Rebound Settings**: AI monitors how the suspension compresses and rebounds during practice runs, identifying the ideal balance for each track.
- **Real-Time Data Analysis**: Sensors mounted on the forks and rear shock provide data on impact forces, rider weight distribution, and terrain feedback, allowing for instant adjustments.
- **Personalized Recommendations**: AI takes into account a rider's style, weight, and typical speed to customize suspension settings for maximum comfort and control.

For example, if a rider is consistently bottoming out during landings, the AI system might suggest increasing the suspension's compression damping or adjusting the spring preload.

2. Optimizing Tire Performance

Tires are the only point of contact between the bike and the track, making their optimization crucial. AI tools ensure that tires perform optimally by analyzing data on grip, pressure, and wear.

- **Tire Pressure Optimization**: AI systems equipped with pressure sensors adjust tire pressure in real-time based on terrain and weather conditions, ensuring maximum traction and stability.
- **Grip Analysis**: By monitoring wheel slippage and traction during practice runs, AI helps riders select the best tire compounds for specific track surfaces, such as hard-packed dirt or loose sand.
- **Wear Prediction**: AI can forecast tire wear over a race or practice session, alerting riders to replace tires before performance deteriorates.

AI-driven tire optimization reduces the guesswork involved in selecting and maintaining tires, giving riders a competitive edge.

3. Integrating Suspension and Tire Data

The synergy between suspension and tire performance is critical for overall bike handling. AI platforms integrate data from both systems to recommend holistic adjustments. For instance:

- If AI detects excessive wheel bounce during cornering, it might suggest a combination of suspension tweaks and tire pressure adjustments.
- Riders receive actionable insights to achieve better handling, reduced lap times, and improved race-day confidence.

Adapting Engine Settings Based on Terrain Data

A motocross bike's engine must deliver optimal power and responsiveness to handle various terrains effectively. AI-powered tools have made it possible to customize engine settings with incredible precision, tailoring performance to the specific demands of each track.

1. Terrain Mapping and Data Analysis

AI systems use advanced mapping and data analysis to understand the unique characteristics of different tracks. Key processes include:

- **Terrain Scanning**: Drones or onboard cameras equipped with AI algorithms create detailed 3D maps of the track, identifying features like jumps, corners, and elevation changes.
- **Surface Analysis**: AI assesses the composition of the track surface—whether it's sandy, muddy, or hard-packed—and predicts how it will affect engine performance.

These insights enable riders to fine-tune their engine settings for optimal performance on any terrain.

2. Customizing Power Delivery

AI tools allow riders to adjust their bike's power delivery to match the terrain. Customizations include:

- **Throttle Response**: AI adjusts throttle mapping to provide smoother acceleration on loose or slippery surfaces, reducing the risk of wheelspin.
- **Torque Optimization**: For tracks with steep inclines or heavy mud, AI enhances low-end torque to improve traction and control.
- **RPM Adjustments**: AI optimizes RPM limits to balance power output and fuel efficiency, ensuring the bike performs consistently throughout the race.

For example, if a track includes a mix of tight corners and long straights, the AI system might recommend a throttle map that provides aggressive acceleration on the straights but smoother power delivery in the corners.

3. Dynamic Tuning During Races

Some advanced AI systems can make real-time engine adjustments during a race. By monitoring factors like rider inputs and track conditions, these systems optimize performance on the fly. Benefits include:

- **Fuel Efficiency**: AI manages fuel injection to ensure the bike completes the race without running out of fuel.
- **Heat Management**: By adjusting engine timing and cooling systems, AI prevents overheating during intense races.
- **Enhanced Stability**: AI minimizes engine braking to improve stability during descents or tight cornering.

These dynamic adjustments give riders a significant advantage, particularly in unpredictable race conditions.

Predictive Adjustments for Weather and Track Conditions

Weather and track conditions can change rapidly during a motocross race, creating challenges for riders and teams. AI's predictive capabilities enable proactive adjustments, ensuring bikes remain competitive regardless of external factors.

1. Weather Forecasting for Race Preparation

AI-powered weather forecasting tools provide detailed predictions on temperature, humidity, wind speed, and precipitation. Teams use this information to prepare their bikes accordingly.

- **Rainy Conditions**: AI recommends softer suspension settings and tire compounds with deeper treads to enhance grip.
- **Hot Weather**: AI suggests adjustments to cooling systems and tire pressures to prevent overheating or blowouts.
- **Windy Conditions**: By analyzing wind direction and speed, AI helps riders adjust their racing lines to minimize drag and maintain stability.

For example, if heavy rain is expected during a race, the AI system might advise switching to rain-specific tires and adjusting the suspension to handle slippery conditions.

2. Adapting to Track Changes

Tracks can evolve significantly over the course of a race, as riders create ruts, displace dirt, and alter the surface. AI tools analyze these changes in real-time to provide actionable recommendations.

- **Rider Lines**: AI identifies the fastest and safest lines through the track as conditions change.
- **Suspension Adjustments**: Based on track roughness, AI might suggest softening the suspension to improve comfort and control.
- **Tire Pressure Modifications**: AI adjusts tire pressure to maintain optimal grip as the track becomes more compacted or loosened.

These insights allow riders to adapt quickly, maintaining their competitive edge throughout the race.

3. Combining Weather and Track Data for Holistic Adjustments

AI systems integrate weather and track data to provide comprehensive recommendations. For instance:

- If a track becomes muddy due to sudden rain, AI might suggest reducing tire pressure, softening suspension, and adjusting engine torque for better traction.
- By considering multiple variables simultaneously, AI ensures that every adjustment contributes to overall performance.

This holistic approach ensures that riders can respond effectively to unpredictable conditions, maximizing their chances of success.

Customizing bikes for peak performance has never been more precise or efficient, thanks to the integration of AI technologies. By optimizing suspension and tires, adapting engine settings to terrain data, and making predictive adjustments for weather and track conditions, AI empowers riders to tackle any challenge with confidence.

These advancements not only enhance bike performance but also improve rider safety, reduce maintenance costs, and provide a competitive edge in an increasingly demanding sport. As AI continues to evolve, its role in motocross will only grow, transforming how riders and teams approach preparation, strategy, and performance on the track.

Section 3: Enhancing Safety Through AI

Safety is paramount in motocross racing, where riders face intense physical demands, unpredictable terrains, and high-speed maneuvers. Despite the thrill of the sport, the risk of accidents and injuries looms large, making safety enhancements a critical area of focus. Artificial intelligence (AI) has emerged as a game-changer, providing innovative tools to enhance rider safety on and off the track. This section explores how AI-powered crash prediction and avoidance systems, tools for monitoring rider safety, and real-time alerts for bike and rider risks are revolutionizing safety in motocross.

Crash Prediction and Avoidance Systems

One of the most significant advancements in AI for motocross safety is the development of crash prediction and avoidance systems. These technologies analyze vast amounts of data to predict potential accidents and help riders avoid dangerous situations.

1. AI-Driven Risk Assessment Models

AI systems utilize machine learning algorithms to predict crash risks by analyzing historical and real-time data from races and practice sessions.

- **Terrain Analysis**: AI evaluates track conditions, such as loose gravel, steep inclines, or sudden drops, to identify high-risk areas.
- **Speed and Trajectory Monitoring**: By analyzing a rider's speed, trajectory, and lean angle, AI predicts scenarios where a crash is likely to occur, such as over-leaning in a corner or misjudging a jump.
- **Weather Impact**: AI incorporates weather data, such as rain or wind, to forecast how environmental factors might increase crash risks.

For example, if a rider approaches a corner too fast on a wet track, the AI system can alert the rider to slow down or adjust their line to reduce the risk of sliding out.

2. Collision Avoidance Technologies

AI-powered sensors and cameras integrated into bikes can detect potential collisions with other riders or obstacles.

- **Proximity Alerts**: Sensors monitor the distance between bikes, warning riders if they are too close to others.
- **Obstacle Detection**: Cameras and AI algorithms identify obstacles on the track, such as debris or unexpected changes in terrain, and provide timely alerts.
- **Brake Assistance**: In critical situations, AI systems can activate or recommend braking to help riders avoid collisions.

These technologies not only reduce the likelihood of accidents but also instill confidence in riders, allowing them to focus more on their performance.

3. Predictive Injury Prevention

AI systems go beyond crash avoidance by predicting potential injuries based on rider data.

- **Fatigue Monitoring**: By analyzing physiological data, such as heart rate and muscle strain, AI can identify when a rider is fatigued and at greater risk of making mistakes.
- **Impact Prediction**: AI models simulate the effects of potential crashes, helping riders and teams understand how to minimize the severity of impacts through protective gear or bike adjustments.

The ability to predict and prevent crashes and injuries represents a monumental step forward in motocross safety.

AI-Enabled Tools for Monitoring Rider Safety

In addition to preventing crashes, AI plays a vital role in monitoring rider safety during races and training sessions. Advanced tools equipped with AI technology provide real-time insights into a rider's physical condition and performance.

1. Wearable Devices for Health Monitoring

AI-powered wearables are increasingly popular in motocross, offering continuous monitoring of vital signs and physical metrics.

- **Heart Rate and Oxygen Levels**: Sensors track a rider's heart rate and oxygen saturation, ensuring they remain within safe limits during intense races.
- **Hydration Levels**: AI algorithms analyze sweat data to detect dehydration, which can impair performance and increase the risk of accidents.
- **Muscle Fatigue Detection**: By monitoring muscle activity, wearables alert riders when they are at risk of overexertion or injury.

For example, if a rider's heart rate spikes beyond a safe threshold during a race, the AI system can recommend a short recovery period to prevent heat exhaustion or cardiac stress.

2. Helmet-Mounted AI Systems

Helmets equipped with AI technology offer additional safety features, such as:

- **Impact Sensors**: Detecting the force of impacts during crashes and assessing the likelihood of concussions or other injuries.
- **Augmented Reality Displays**: Providing riders with critical information, such as track conditions and upcoming obstacles, without distracting them from the race.
- **Voice-Activated Assistance**: Enabling riders to receive safety alerts or communicate with their teams hands-free.

These helmet-mounted systems not only protect riders during accidents but also enhance their situational awareness on the track.

3. AI Platforms for Long-Term Safety Analysis

Beyond real-time monitoring, AI platforms analyze data over time to identify trends and make recommendations for improved safety.

- **Injury Pattern Analysis**: AI identifies common causes of injuries, helping riders and teams address underlying issues, such as improper technique or equipment.
- **Customized Safety Plans**: Based on individual data, AI creates personalized safety strategies, including training modifications and gear recommendations.
- **Preventative Measures**: AI highlights potential risks before they become problems, allowing riders to proactively address safety concerns.

These tools empower riders to take control of their safety, both on and off the track.

Real-Time Alerts for Bike and Rider Risks

AI's ability to deliver real-time alerts is one of its most valuable contributions to motocross safety. By providing instant feedback on bike performance and rider conditions, AI ensures that potential risks are addressed immediately.

1. Bike Performance Monitoring

AI systems continuously monitor key aspects of bike performance to detect issues that could compromise safety.

- **Engine Temperature and Performance**: AI alerts riders if the engine overheats or underperforms, preventing potential breakdowns or accidents.
- **Brake Efficiency**: Sensors monitor brake wear and effectiveness, warning riders if the brakes need adjustment or replacement.

- **Suspension Health**: AI evaluates suspension performance in real-time, ensuring it provides adequate support and stability.

For instance, if a suspension component begins to fail during a race, the AI system can alert the rider to adjust their speed or return to the pit for repairs.

2. Rider Risk Detection

AI also monitors rider behavior and physical condition to identify risks.

- **Sudden Movements**: AI detects abrupt or erratic movements, such as unexpected swerves or loss of control, and alerts the rider to regain stability.
- **Posture Analysis**: Cameras and sensors analyze the rider's posture, ensuring proper form and reducing the risk of strain or injury.
- **Stress Indicators**: By analyzing voice patterns or physiological data, AI identifies signs of stress or panic, helping riders stay calm and focused.

These alerts help riders make quick, informed decisions that enhance their safety on the track.

3. Team Communication and Support

AI-powered communication systems enable teams to provide real-time support to riders during races.

- **Track Updates**: Teams can relay information about changing track conditions or hazards, giving riders a tactical advantage.
- **Strategy Adjustments**: AI provides teams with data-driven insights, allowing them to suggest adjustments to a rider's approach or pace.
- **Emergency Response**: In the event of an accident, AI systems notify medical personnel with precise location and injury data, ensuring a swift response.

The integration of AI into team communication systems creates a seamless flow of information, enhancing both performance and safety.

The integration of AI into motocross has significantly elevated safety standards, addressing the sport's inherent risks with innovative solutions. From crash prediction and avoidance systems to AI-enabled tools for monitoring rider safety and real-time alerts for bike and rider risks, these technologies have transformed how riders and teams approach safety.

As AI continues to evolve, its potential to enhance safety in motocross is limitless. Future advancements may include fully autonomous safety systems, enhanced injury prevention technologies, and even AI-driven medical diagnostics for post-race care. By embracing these innovations, motocross can remain an exhilarating yet safer sport for riders of all skill levels.

Chapter 4: AI and Track Analysis

Section 1: Understanding Track Dynamics

In motocross, understanding the nuances of a track is crucial to achieving optimal performance. Tracks are dynamic environments with constantly changing conditions, making them a challenge for even the most skilled riders. Advances in artificial intelligence (AI) and data collection tools, such as drones, have provided motocross teams with powerful ways to map tracks, analyze surface variability, and visualize challenges in detail. These innovations allow riders to adapt their strategies and perform with greater precision. In this section, we'll explore how drones and AI are used to map tracks, methods for collecting data on track surface variability, and how AI tools visualize track challenges.

Using Drones and AI to Map Tracks

One of the most transformative applications of AI in motocross is the use of drones to create detailed track maps. These aerial devices, combined with AI technology, allow teams to capture high-resolution imagery and construct accurate digital models of tracks.

1. High-Resolution Track Mapping

Drones equipped with advanced cameras and sensors can fly over motocross tracks to capture detailed images and videos.

- **3D Mapping**: AI-powered software processes these images to create three-dimensional models of the track, highlighting elevation changes, curves, and obstacles.
- **Topographic Analysis**: Drones collect data on the terrain's elevation and slope, providing valuable insights into how the track will challenge riders.
- **Dynamic Updates**: For tracks that change frequently due to weather or maintenance, drones can provide updated maps before each race.

For example, a track with steep hills and sharp turns might pose unique challenges, and drone-generated maps allow riders to study these elements in advance, optimizing their approach.

2. Identifying Hazard Zones

Drones also help identify potential hazard zones on a track.

- **Obstacle Detection**: AI algorithms analyze footage to pinpoint areas with debris, ruts, or other obstacles that could pose risks.
- **Water Accumulation**: After rainfall, drones can identify sections of the track prone to water pooling, enabling teams to plan accordingly.
- **Blind Spots**: Drones provide aerial views that highlight sections of the track with limited visibility, allowing riders to anticipate these challenges.

By identifying hazards in advance, riders can adjust their strategies to minimize risks and maximize their performance.

3. Efficiency in Track Mapping

The combination of drones and AI significantly reduces the time and effort required to analyze a track.

- **Automated Processes**: Drones operate autonomously, capturing data without requiring extensive manual input.
- **Rapid Analysis**: AI processes the collected data in real time, providing actionable insights within minutes.
- **Cost-Effective Solutions**: Compared to traditional track analysis methods, drones offer a more affordable and efficient option for teams and organizers.

These advantages make drone-based track mapping a standard practice in modern motocross.

Collecting Data on Track Surface Variability

The variability of track surfaces in motocross is a defining characteristic that impacts rider performance and bike handling. AI-powered tools and sensors allow teams to gather detailed data on these variations, enabling better preparation and decision-making.

1. Understanding Surface Types

Tracks often feature a mix of surfaces, such as dirt, sand, gravel, and clay, each of which affects traction and bike stability.

- **Material Composition Analysis**: AI tools analyze samples from different sections of the track to determine the composition and density of the surface materials.
- **Traction Coefficients**: By studying the interaction between tires and the surface, AI calculates traction levels for various conditions, such as wet or dry terrain.
- **Erosion Patterns**: AI predicts how the surface will change over time due to wear and weather, helping riders anticipate future challenges.

For instance, a section of the track with loose sand may require adjustments to bike suspension and tire pressure for optimal performance.

2. Real-Time Surface Monitoring

Sensors embedded in the track or attached to bikes provide real-time data on surface conditions.

- **Grip Levels**: AI measures grip levels to assess how well tires adhere to the track under specific conditions.
- **Temperature Effects**: Surface temperature data is analyzed to determine how heat impacts traction and bike performance.

- **Dynamic Changes**: During races, AI tracks how the surface evolves, such as the formation of ruts or the drying of wet patches.

This data allows teams to make quick adjustments, such as changing tire compounds or suspension settings, to adapt to shifting conditions.

3. Predicting Surface Challenges

AI excels at predicting how track surfaces will behave under different scenarios, providing a competitive edge.

- **Weather Forecast Integration**: By combining track data with weather forecasts, AI predicts how rain, wind, or heat will alter surface conditions.
- **Usage Impact**: AI models simulate how repeated use during practice sessions and races will affect the track, such as increased rut depth or compaction.
- **Customized Recommendations**: Based on these predictions, AI suggests strategies for riders, such as selecting specific lines or adjusting throttle control.

Predictive insights empower riders to anticipate challenges and maintain consistent performance throughout a race.

Visualizing Track Challenges Through AI Tools

Visualizing track challenges is a critical aspect of race preparation. AI tools transform raw data into intuitive visual representations that help riders and teams understand track dynamics and develop effective strategies.

1. Heatmaps for Track Analysis

AI-generated heatmaps provide a visual representation of critical areas on the track.

- **High-Risk Zones**: Heatmaps highlight sections with a high likelihood of accidents or difficulty, such as sharp turns or steep descents.
- **Optimal Racing Lines**: By analyzing past performance data, AI identifies the fastest and safest lines for each section of the track.
- **Traffic Flow Analysis**: Heatmaps show areas where riders are likely to bunch up, helping teams strategize overtaking opportunities.

These visualizations simplify complex data, allowing riders to focus on actionable insights.

2. Virtual Track Walks

AI-powered virtual reality (VR) and augmented reality (AR) tools offer riders an immersive way to familiarize themselves with a track.

- **Pre-Race Familiarization**: Riders can "walk" the track in a virtual environment, studying its features and challenges in detail.

- **Scenario Simulations**: AI simulates different scenarios, such as racing in wet conditions or avoiding obstacles, to prepare riders for various possibilities.
- **Interactive Feedback**: Virtual tools provide real-time feedback on a rider's approach to specific sections, suggesting improvements.

Virtual track walks give riders a competitive advantage by allowing them to mentally and physically prepare for the race.

3. AI-Driven Strategy Development

AI tools also assist teams in developing comprehensive strategies based on track analysis.

- **Line Selection Models**: AI suggests the best lines for different sections, considering factors like rider skill and bike setup.
- **Pace Recommendations**: By analyzing track conditions, AI provides guidance on optimal lap times and pacing strategies.
- **Competitor Analysis**: AI evaluates the performance of competitors on the same track, identifying strengths and weaknesses to exploit during the race.

These strategic insights enhance team preparation and rider confidence, leading to better results on race day.

Understanding track dynamics is a fundamental aspect of motocross racing, and AI has revolutionized how riders and teams approach this challenge. From using drones to map tracks and collecting detailed data on surface variability to visualizing track challenges through advanced tools, AI provides unparalleled insights that enhance preparation and performance.

As AI technology continues to evolve, its applications in track analysis are expected to become even more sophisticated. Future developments may include autonomous drones for continuous track monitoring, real-time 4D simulations, and AI-powered coaching systems that adapt strategies mid-race. By embracing these innovations, motocross can maintain its status as an exhilarating and competitive sport while minimizing risks and maximizing performance.

Section 2: Strategic Race Planning

Strategic race planning is one of the most critical aspects of motocross racing. The ability to anticipate track dynamics, predict competitors' moves, and make in-race adjustments often separates winning riders from the rest of the pack. The integration of artificial intelligence (AI) into this domain has transformed how riders and their teams approach race strategy. By leveraging AI-powered tools, riders can identify the best lines for maximum speed, adapt strategies based on competitor data, and make real-time adjustments during races. This section explores these points in detail and demonstrates how AI is revolutionizing motocross strategy.

Predicting the Best Lines for Maximum Speed

One of the most crucial elements of motocross race planning is identifying and sticking to the optimal racing line. The racing line is the path a rider takes around the track that minimizes lap time while maximizing control. AI has become a powerful tool for determining these optimal lines, enabling riders to achieve peak performance.

1. Analyzing Track Data

AI-powered tools use a combination of drone footage, GPS data, and sensor inputs to analyze the track in detail.

- **Elevation and Gradient Analysis**: AI evaluates changes in elevation and slope to determine which lines offer the best combination of speed and stability. For example, a steeper descent might require a wider approach to maintain control.
- **Cornering Dynamics**: AI identifies the best approach and exit angles for corners, factoring in the rider's speed, bike setup, and track conditions.
- **Surface Conditions**: By analyzing surface grip levels, AI can recommend lines that minimize the risk of skidding or losing traction.

For instance, on a track with loose dirt and sharp turns, AI might suggest a slightly slower approach to maintain traction, followed by a burst of acceleration upon exiting the corner.

2. Simulating Multiple Scenarios

AI-powered simulation tools allow teams to model various scenarios to test different lines.

- **Optimal Speed Profiles**: Simulations calculate the ideal speed for each section of the track based on the chosen line.
- **Risk Assessment**: AI evaluates the risks associated with each line, such as proximity to obstacles or potential for collisions with other riders.
- **Adaptability Testing**: Teams can simulate how different weather or track conditions impact the effectiveness of a line.

These simulations help riders prepare for a wide range of possibilities, ensuring they're ready to adapt as conditions change during the race.

3. Real-Time Line Adjustments

During a race, AI systems can provide real-time feedback on line selection.

- **Wearable Displays**: Riders equipped with wearable devices receive suggestions for line adjustments based on evolving track conditions.
- **Dynamic Updates**: AI tracks changes such as the formation of ruts or water accumulation and recommends alternate lines to avoid these hazards.
- **Competitor Influence**: AI also considers the movements of other riders when suggesting adjustments, helping riders avoid crowded or blocked lines.

This real-time guidance enables riders to maintain maximum speed and efficiency throughout the race.

Adapting Race Strategy Based on Competitor Data

In addition to understanding the track, riders must account for the strategies and behaviors of their competitors. AI excels at analyzing competitor data and providing actionable insights to help riders gain an edge.

1. Competitor Profiling

AI systems can analyze historical data on competitors to identify patterns and tendencies.

- **Performance Metrics**: By studying past race results, AI assesses a competitor's strengths and weaknesses, such as their cornering speed or straight-line acceleration.
- **Preferred Lines**: AI identifies the lines that competitors are most likely to take based on their riding style and past behavior.
- **Behavior Under Pressure**: AI evaluates how competitors respond in high-pressure situations, such as overtaking attempts or battling for the lead.

For example, if a competitor tends to struggle in technical sections, AI might suggest attacking in those areas to gain an advantage.

2. Real-Time Competitor Tracking

During a race, AI systems provide real-time updates on the positions and actions of competitors.

- **GPS Monitoring**: By tracking the GPS signals of all riders, AI creates a live map of the race, showing where competitors are gaining or losing time.
- **Performance Comparisons**: AI compares a rider's lap times, cornering speeds, and other metrics to those of their competitors to identify opportunities for improvement.
- **Predictive Overtaking Opportunities**: By analyzing speed differentials and track positioning, AI predicts the best moments for overtaking.

These insights allow riders to adjust their strategies dynamically, ensuring they stay competitive throughout the race.

3. Strategic Team Communication

AI also facilitates better communication between riders and their teams.

- **Data-Driven Advice**: Teams use AI insights to provide riders with specific instructions, such as when to push harder or conserve energy.
- **Competitor Warnings**: AI alerts teams to potential threats, such as a fast-approaching competitor or an impending battle for position.
- **End-of-Race Planning**: Based on real-time competitor data, AI helps teams plan their final laps to maximize their chances of success.

This collaborative approach ensures that riders and teams are always on the same page, making split-second decisions with confidence.

Leveraging AI Insights for In-Race Adjustments

No matter how well a race is planned, unforeseen circumstances can arise, requiring riders to adapt on the fly. AI plays a crucial role in enabling these in-race adjustments, providing riders with the information they need to make quick and effective decisions.

1. Monitoring Race Dynamics

AI systems continuously monitor the race to identify changes that require immediate action.

- **Track Condition Changes**: If the track becomes wet or rutted during the race, AI alerts riders to adjust their speed or line accordingly.
- **Bike Performance Issues**: AI systems monitor the bike's health and alert riders to potential problems, such as tire wear or overheating.
- **Competitor Positioning**: AI tracks the movements of competitors, identifying opportunities to overtake or defend a position.

These insights ensure that riders are always aware of their surroundings and can react proactively.

2. Adaptive Riding Recommendations

AI tools provide riders with adaptive recommendations to help them navigate unexpected challenges.

- **Throttle and Brake Adjustments**: AI suggests changes to throttle or brake inputs to optimize performance in specific sections of the track.
- **Suspension Tuning**: On advanced bikes, AI systems can make real-time adjustments to suspension settings based on track conditions.
- **Energy Management**: AI advises riders on when to conserve energy and when to push harder, helping them maintain peak performance throughout the race.

For example, if a rider is approaching a technical section after a long straight, AI might recommend a specific braking point to maximize cornering efficiency.

3. Enhancing Rider Confidence

Perhaps one of the most significant benefits of AI in in-race adjustments is the confidence it provides to riders.

- **Reduced Uncertainty**: With AI handling the analysis of track and competitor data, riders can focus solely on their performance.
- **Improved Decision-Making**: Riders receive clear, actionable insights that simplify complex decisions.
- **Real-Time Feedback Loops**: The constant flow of information ensures that riders are always aware of their performance and can make continuous improvements.

This confidence often translates into better results, as riders are free to focus on their skills without being distracted by external factors.

Strategic race planning has always been a cornerstone of motocross success, and AI has elevated it to new heights. By predicting the best lines for maximum speed, adapting strategies based on competitor data, and enabling real-time in-race adjustments, AI provides riders and teams with a significant competitive edge.

As AI technology continues to advance, its applications in motocross strategy will only grow more sophisticated. Future innovations may include fully autonomous strategy assistants, real-time AI-driven coaching systems, and enhanced collaboration tools that seamlessly integrate riders, teams, and data.

For riders who embrace these tools, the rewards are clear: faster lap times, smarter strategies, and greater confidence on the track. By combining human skill with AI precision, motocross is poised to become even more thrilling and competitive in the years to come.

Section 3: Post-Race Analytics

Post-race analysis is an essential part of a rider's improvement journey in motocross. The ability to assess performance, identify strengths and weaknesses, and implement changes for future races is what separates good riders from great ones. With the integration of artificial intelligence (AI), post-race analytics has evolved into a data-driven process that offers unprecedented insights. This section explores how AI helps riders review performance metrics, pinpoint areas for improvement, and apply these insights to their next race plans.

Reviewing Performance Metrics After a Race

AI technology has revolutionized how performance metrics are reviewed after a motocross race. By collecting vast amounts of data during the event, AI systems provide detailed reports that help riders and teams understand every aspect of the race.

1. Collecting and Organizing Race Data

AI systems gather data from various sources to create a comprehensive picture of the race.

- **Wearable Sensors**: Devices worn by riders collect information on heart rate, reaction times, and physical exertion throughout the race.
- **On-Bike Sensors**: These sensors monitor key metrics like throttle usage, braking patterns, suspension performance, and tire traction.
- **Track Data**: AI systems analyze track conditions, line choices, and lap times to evaluate how the rider interacted with the terrain.

For example, if a rider consistently lost time in specific corners, the data might show excessive braking or poor line selection, helping the team identify the root cause.

2. Visualizing Race Performance

AI systems transform raw data into intuitive visualizations that are easy to understand.

- **Heat Maps**: These maps highlight the rider's performance across different sections of the track, showing where they gained or lost time.
- **Performance Graphs**: Graphs illustrate trends like lap time consistency, speed fluctuations, and gear usage.
- **Comparative Analysis**: AI compares the rider's performance to competitors, highlighting areas where they outperformed or lagged behind.

For instance, a heat map might reveal that a rider consistently lost speed on uphill sections, suggesting the need for adjustments to throttle control or bike setup.

3. Creating Summary Reports

At the end of the race, AI generates detailed reports summarizing key performance metrics.

- **Lap-by-Lap Analysis**: A breakdown of each lap, including time, speed, and cornering efficiency.
- **Mechanical Performance**: Insights into how the bike performed under race conditions, including any signs of wear or mechanical stress.
- **Rider Efficiency**: Metrics on physical exertion, energy use, and reaction times.

These reports provide a starting point for deeper analysis, enabling teams to prioritize areas for improvement.

Identifying Areas for Improvement Using AI Reports

The detailed insights provided by AI reports make it easier to identify specific areas where riders and their bikes can improve. By focusing on these areas, teams can make targeted changes that lead to better results in future races.

1. Pinpointing Rider Weaknesses

AI systems analyze rider behavior to uncover weaknesses that may have gone unnoticed.

- **Cornering Techniques**: If a rider consistently struggles in corners, AI might identify issues with braking points, lean angles, or throttle application.
- **Line Selection**: AI highlights suboptimal line choices, showing how alternative lines could have saved time.
- **Fatigue Patterns**: Wearable data reveals when and where the rider began to tire, helping teams address endurance training.

For example, if a rider's performance dropped in the final laps, the AI report might suggest a need for improved stamina or better energy management during the race.

2. Evaluating Bike Performance

AI diagnostics help teams identify mechanical issues or inefficiencies in the bike's setup.

- **Suspension Settings**: If the bike's suspension didn't perform well on rough sections, AI might recommend adjustments to damping or spring rates.
- **Tire Performance**: AI analyzes tire wear and grip levels, suggesting changes to tire choice or pressure for similar conditions.
- **Engine Optimization**: Reports on engine performance, including power delivery and fuel efficiency, highlight opportunities for tuning.

For instance, if the bike struggled to maintain speed on straight sections, AI might recommend changes to the gear ratio or engine mapping.

3. Assessing Strategy Effectiveness

AI evaluates how well the rider's strategy worked during the race, providing actionable feedback.

- **Start Performance**: Insights into how quickly the rider got off the line and positioned themselves in the pack.
- **Overtaking Opportunities**: Analysis of successful and missed overtaking attempts, along with suggestions for improvement.
- **Defensive Tactics**: Evaluation of how effectively the rider defended their position against competitors.

These strategic insights help teams refine their approach, ensuring the rider is better prepared for similar scenarios in the future.

Applying Insights to the Next Race Plan

The ultimate goal of post-race analysis is to use the insights gained to improve future performance. AI systems play a key role in translating data into actionable strategies, enabling riders and teams to continuously evolve.

1. Developing Targeted Training Programs

Based on the weaknesses identified in the AI report, teams can create personalized training plans.

- **Skill Drills**: Focused exercises to improve specific skills, such as cornering or throttle control.
- **Endurance Training**: Programs to build stamina and reduce fatigue during long races.
- **Mental Preparation**: Techniques to address stress or improve focus in high-pressure situations.

For example, if a rider struggled with reaction times during starts, their training might include practice starts with AI-provided feedback on timing and technique.

2. Optimizing Bike Setup

AI insights guide teams in making adjustments to the bike for the next race.

- **Track-Specific Tuning**: Changes to suspension, tires, and engine settings based on the conditions expected at the next track.
- **Preventative Maintenance**: Replacing or repairing components flagged by AI diagnostics as potential weak points.
- **Experimental Upgrades**: Testing new parts or settings recommended by AI simulations for improved performance.

By addressing the issues highlighted in the post-race analysis, teams ensure the bike is in peak condition for the next event.

3. Refining Race Strategy

AI helps teams create more effective race strategies by learning from past mistakes and successes.

- **Track Insights**: Using data from previous races to plan the best lines and approaches for the next track.
- **Competitor Analysis**: Factoring in updated insights on competitors to anticipate their moves.
- **Dynamic Planning**: Preparing contingency plans for various scenarios, such as changes in weather or unexpected track conditions.

For instance, if a rider struggled to overtake competitors in the last race, AI might recommend a more aggressive strategy or identify specific sections of the track where overtaking is easier.

Post-race analytics is a vital component of motocross success, and AI has elevated it to new levels of precision and effectiveness. By reviewing performance metrics, identifying areas for improvement, and applying these insights to future races, riders and teams can achieve continuous progress.

AI's ability to analyze vast amounts of data and provide actionable recommendations ensures that no detail is overlooked. From refining riding techniques to optimizing bike setups and crafting smarter race strategies, AI empowers riders to reach their full potential.

As motocross continues to evolve, the role of AI in post-race analysis will only grow more important. Future advancements may include even more sophisticated tools for data collection, real-time insights during races, and fully integrated systems that streamline the entire feedback loop. By embracing these technologies, riders and teams can stay ahead of the competition and achieve greater success on the track.

Chapter 5: AI for Competitive Advantage

Section 1: Leveraging Data from Competitors

In the high-stakes world of motocross, gaining an edge over competitors can make the difference between victory and defeat. The integration of artificial intelligence (AI) into the sport has transformed how riders and teams approach this challenge. One of AI's most impactful applications is its ability to study rival performance, identify weaknesses, and anticipate opponent strategies. By leveraging AI tools and insights, riders can develop informed race plans that put them ahead of the competition. This section delves into how AI enables teams to gain a competitive advantage by analyzing their rivals.

AI Tools to Study Rival Performance

AI has revolutionized how teams gather and process information about competitors, offering detailed insights that were once unimaginable.

1. Video Analysis Using AI

One of the most common ways teams study rivals is through video analysis.

- **Tracking Techniques**: AI-powered video analysis tools can break down a competitor's racing technique, including their cornering speed, acceleration patterns, and throttle control.
- **Performance Heatmaps**: By analyzing footage of multiple laps, AI generates heatmaps showing where a rider performs exceptionally well or struggles on the track.
- **Automated Tagging**: Advanced systems automatically tag key events, such as overtakes, braking points, or mistakes, allowing teams to focus on critical moments.

For instance, software like Hudl or Dartfish has been adapted for motocross, enabling teams to create a comprehensive picture of a rival's racing style.

2. Telemetry and Sensor Data Analysis

In professional motocross, many competitors use telemetry and sensor-equipped bikes. While these systems are designed for internal use, teams can often gather external data during races.

- **Speed and Acceleration**: AI tools track a rival's speed in various sections of the track, providing insights into their strengths and weaknesses.
- **Braking Patterns**: By studying how and when a competitor brakes, teams can learn about their approach to corners and jumps.
- **Suspension Behavior**: Analyzing how a rival's bike handles rough terrain can reveal their suspension setup and its advantages.

Some systems, such as GPS-based tools, allow teams to track competitors in real-time during races, adding an extra layer of analysis.

3. AI-Driven Competitor Profiles

AI can aggregate data from various sources—race results, training sessions, and even social media—to create detailed profiles of competitors.

- **Consistency Metrics**: Insights into a rider's lap time consistency and performance under pressure.
- **Track Preferences**: Analysis of how a competitor performs on different track types or weather conditions.
- **Historical Trends**: Identifying patterns in a rival's performance over time, such as improvement areas or recurring mistakes.

For example, if a rival consistently struggles with muddy tracks, this information can inform strategic decisions during wet-weather races.

Gaining Insights into Competitor Weaknesses

Understanding a competitor's weaknesses is a crucial part of building an effective race strategy. AI provides an objective, data-driven approach to identifying and exploiting these vulnerabilities.

1. Spotting Inconsistencies

AI tools excel at identifying inconsistencies in a competitor's performance.

- **Lap Time Variability**: Riders who struggle to maintain consistent lap times are more likely to falter under pressure.
- **Fatigue Patterns**: Wearable data or race footage can reveal when a rival begins to tire, often during the final laps of a race.
- **Mistake-Prone Areas**: AI highlights sections of the track where a competitor frequently makes mistakes, such as missing apexes or losing traction.

For instance, if a rider routinely loses time in tight corners, teams can plan overtaking maneuvers in these areas.

2. Analyzing Equipment Limitations

AI tools also provide insights into a competitor's bike setup, which can reveal limitations.

- **Tire Wear**: Observing how a rival's tires perform over a race can indicate whether they struggle with grip or durability.
- **Suspension Issues**: AI analysis of jumps and rough sections may show that a competitor's suspension is suboptimal, affecting their speed and control.
- **Engine Performance**: By comparing acceleration and top speed, teams can infer the power and tuning of a rival's engine.

For example, if a competitor's bike struggles on uphill sections, this may indicate insufficient torque or improper gearing.

3. Identifying Strategic Vulnerabilities

AI doesn't just analyze physical performance—it also evaluates a competitor's strategic decisions.

- **Start-Line Behavior**: Analyzing how a rival positions themselves at the start can reveal hesitations or weaknesses in their approach.
- **Overtaking Patterns**: Teams can study how a competitor attempts overtakes, including their timing and success rate.
- **Defensive Techniques**: Understanding how a rival defends their position can help teams plan effective attacks.

For instance, if a competitor tends to defend aggressively on straights but leaves corners exposed, teams can target these weaknesses.

Anticipating Opponent Strategies

In addition to analyzing past performance, AI excels at predicting how competitors are likely to approach future races. This predictive capability is invaluable for staying one step ahead.

1. Forecasting Race Tactics

AI uses historical data to predict a rival's race strategy.

- **Preferred Lines**: By studying previous races on the same track, AI identifies the lines a competitor is most likely to choose.
- **Overtaking Zones**: Predicting where a rival is likely to attempt overtakes based on their past behavior.
- **Pacing Strategy**: Insights into whether a competitor prefers to start aggressively or conserve energy for later laps.

For example, if a rival consistently pushes hard in the first few laps, teams can plan to counter this early aggression with defensive tactics.

2. Preparing for Psychological Play

Motocross is as much a mental game as a physical one. AI helps teams anticipate how competitors might try to gain a psychological advantage.

- **Trash Talk Patterns**: Analyzing social media and interviews for signs of mental strategies aimed at unsettling opponents.
- **Pressure Points**: Identifying scenarios where a rival has previously faltered under pressure, such as critical final laps.
- **Confidence Indicators**: AI evaluates body language, tone, and other subtle cues to gauge a competitor's mindset.

For instance, if a rival seems overly confident before a race, this may signal overambition, which can be exploited with a measured approach.

3. Dynamic In-Race Predictions

AI isn't limited to pre-race analysis—it also provides real-time insights during the race.

- **Live Tracking**: Monitoring a rival's performance in real time to anticipate their next move.
- **Adaptation Alerts**: AI flags changes in a competitor's strategy, such as shifting lines or increasing aggression.
- **Counterstrategy Recommendations**: Suggesting immediate adjustments to counter a rival's tactics.

For example, if a competitor unexpectedly changes their line on a specific section, AI might recommend a different overtaking strategy to stay competitive.

Leveraging AI to study competitors is one of the most effective ways to gain a competitive advantage in motocross. From analyzing rival performance to identifying weaknesses and predicting strategies, AI provides riders and teams with the tools they need to outthink and outperform their opponents.

The ability to collect and process massive amounts of data enables AI to uncover patterns and insights that would otherwise go unnoticed. By combining these insights with strategic planning, riders can approach each race with confidence, knowing they are prepared for whatever their competitors might throw at them.

As AI continues to evolve, its role in competitive analysis will only become more sophisticated. Future advancements may include even more precise tracking, deeper psychological analysis, and fully integrated systems that provide real-time recommendations during races. By embracing these innovations, motocross riders and teams can ensure they stay ahead in an increasingly competitive sport.

Section 2: AI in Team Collaboration

In competitive motocross, every second counts, and teamwork is paramount. From the rider to the coach, mechanics, and pit crew, a successful race relies on seamless collaboration between team members. With the integration of artificial intelligence (AI), these teams can now work more cohesively, make better decisions faster, and stay ahead of the competition. AI is revolutionizing the way data is shared, communication is managed, and race strategies are coordinated—leading to more efficient and effective collaboration. In this section, we'll explore how AI is enhancing team collaboration in the motocross world, focusing on the sharing of data, improving communication, and coordinating pit stops.

Sharing Data Between Riders, Coaches, and Mechanics

In the past, the sharing of critical race data between different members of the motocross team—riders, coaches, and mechanics—was often inefficient and disjointed. However, AI has changed the game, making real-time data sharing more streamlined and actionable.

1. Centralized Data Platforms

AI has enabled the development of centralized data platforms that integrate and process data from various sources, allowing team members to access crucial information in real time.

- **Real-Time Data Sharing**: Through wearable devices and sensors on both riders and bikes, data can be captured continuously during training and races. AI tools like sensors on bikes record performance metrics such as speed, acceleration, suspension behavior, and tire pressure, while wearables track heart rate, fatigue, and stress levels.
- **Integration Across Devices**: AI-enabled platforms synchronize data from multiple sources, allowing riders, coaches, and mechanics to view and analyze the same data. This creates a holistic view of performance, which is particularly valuable when adjustments need to be made mid-race or post-race.
- **Immediate Actionable Insights**: By collecting and analyzing this data in real time, AI provides actionable insights that can be shared across the team. For example, if a rider's heart rate spikes at a certain part of the track, the coach might adjust training to help improve endurance, while mechanics could inspect bike settings that might be contributing to fatigue.

By creating a unified data ecosystem, AI ensures that team members can work with the same set of information, minimizing confusion and optimizing decision-making.

2. Real-Time Tracking and Performance Monitoring

AI allows team members to track performance metrics and monitor rider progress during the race, even when they're not on the track.

- **Telemetry Data**: Telemetry sensors on the rider's bike capture key performance indicators, such as speed, throttle control, suspension settings, and gear usage. Coaches and mechanics can access this data in real time via AI-powered platforms, enabling them to suggest quick adjustments or anticipate potential issues.
- **Wearables for Rider Monitoring**: AI-powered wearables on riders—such as heart rate monitors, GPS trackers, and motion sensors—send data back to the coach and mechanic during training sessions and races. These wearables can monitor the rider's physiological response, track fatigue levels, and help with making decisions on how to tailor training or strategy for the rider.
- **Post-Race Analysis**: After the race, all the gathered data is analyzed by AI to identify strengths and weaknesses. Coaches and mechanics can then collaborate to make changes to bike settings, or adjust the rider's training to address areas that need improvement.

AI ensures that riders, coaches, and mechanics can monitor every element of the race in real time, allowing for better-informed decisions.

Improving Communication Through AI-Powered Platforms

Effective communication between all members of the motocross team is crucial to success. Whether it's the rider needing quick feedback during a race or the mechanic trying to inform the team of a potential bike issue, communication must be both fast and clear. AI is playing a major role in enhancing this communication, making it more efficient and error-free.

1. AI-Driven Messaging and Alerts

In fast-paced environments like motocross, communication between team members needs to be instantaneous. AI-powered messaging and alert systems help ensure that important information is delivered quickly and clearly.

- **Instant Communication Channels**: AI-driven communication platforms allow coaches, mechanics, and the rider to send and receive information with minimal delay. For example, AI-powered systems can send real-time alerts to the rider about track conditions, competitors, or changes in weather, helping the rider stay informed and make strategic decisions.
- **Customizable Alerts**: AI can filter and prioritize alerts based on the importance of the message. For instance, if the mechanic notices a potential mechanical issue during a race, they can send a priority alert to the rider or coach. Alternatively, if there's a slight issue that doesn't need immediate action, the alert can be delayed or logged for later review.
- **Speech-to-Text and Translation Tools**: AI-based speech recognition tools help riders and team members communicate more effectively. For example, speech-to-text technology converts spoken words into text, allowing the rider to relay information about the bike or their condition without taking their hands off the handlebars. AI translation tools can also assist in cross-language communication between teams in international events.

By streamlining communication through AI platforms, teams can reduce the risk of miscommunication and make faster, more informed decisions.

2. Virtual Team Meetings and Strategy Sessions

AI-powered virtual meeting platforms enable teams to collaborate even when they're not physically together. These platforms use AI to facilitate discussions, visualize race strategies, and assess team performance.

- **Race Simulations**: Coaches and mechanics can use AI-driven virtual platforms to simulate various race conditions, strategize, and test different scenarios. This allows the rider to visualize their tactics, review track data, and make adjustments before hitting the track.

- **Strategic Meetings**: AI tools can be used to host strategic meetings with real-time collaboration between riders, mechanics, and coaches. For example, if a rider is struggling with a particular section of the track, the coach can suggest potential adjustments, which are then evaluated by the mechanic for technical feasibility.
- **Video Playback and Analysis**: Teams can replay race footage in virtual meetings, with AI software breaking down key moments, such as overtaking maneuvers, mistakes, or mechanical issues. These meetings can serve as both learning opportunities and strategy planning sessions for future races.

AI-powered virtual platforms make remote collaboration seamless, improving the efficiency of team meetings and enhancing the decision-making process.

Coordinating Pit Stops Using AI Predictions

Pit stops are a critical aspect of motocross racing. The speed and efficiency of a pit stop can significantly influence the outcome of a race, and AI is helping teams optimize this process by providing predictive models and actionable insights.

1. Predictive Maintenance and Stop Planning

AI allows teams to predict when and where a pit stop is most likely needed, based on real-time data.

- **Sensor Data Analysis**: AI tools monitor key components of the bike, such as tire pressure, suspension performance, and engine temperature. This data helps mechanics anticipate when a part might fail or when an adjustment is needed.
- **Fatigue Monitoring for Riders**: AI-powered wearables track a rider's fatigue and stress levels during the race. If the AI system detects signs of excessive fatigue or decreased performance, it can suggest a pit stop or hydration break.
- **Optimal Pit Stop Timing**: AI analyzes race data, including lap times, competitor strategies, and track conditions, to determine the best time for a pit stop. This reduces the chances of an unnecessary stop and ensures that pit crews are ready when needed.

With predictive AI tools, teams can plan pit stops with precision, minimizing delays and maximizing efficiency.

2. AI-Enhanced Pit Crew Coordination

Efficient teamwork in the pit is just as important as the race itself. AI tools help optimize how the pit crew works together to ensure a smooth and quick stop.

- **Task Allocation**: AI can analyze the tasks required during a pit stop, such as tire changes, fuel adjustments, or suspension tweaks, and allocate them to the appropriate team members.

- **Real-Time Decision Making**: AI tools help pit crews make quick decisions during a stop. If a mechanical issue arises unexpectedly, AI systems provide real-time diagnostics and suggest the most efficient course of action.
- **Post-Race Review** After the race, AI software analyzes the efficiency of the pit stop, providing insights into areas for improvement. These data points can then be used to optimize future pit stops.

AI tools ensure that pit crews are well-coordinated and prepared, making the pit stop a seamless part of the race strategy.

AI is reshaping how motocross teams collaborate, providing unprecedented access to data, improving communication, and optimizing pit stop procedures. By integrating AI into every aspect of team operations, teams can make faster, more informed decisions, leading to more effective race strategies and better performance on the track. The ability to share data seamlessly, enhance communication, and coordinate pit stops with precision is giving teams a significant competitive advantage. As AI continues to evolve, it will likely play an even greater role in improving teamwork and enabling riders and their teams to reach new levels of performance.

Section 3: Staying Ahead with Cutting-Edge Tools

In the fast-paced world of professional motocross, staying ahead of the competition is crucial. As technology continues to evolve, artificial intelligence (AI) is becoming an increasingly essential tool for gaining and maintaining a competitive edge. AI can provide valuable insights, optimize performance, and offer predictive capabilities that empower teams and riders to stay ahead of their rivals. In this section, we will explore the emerging AI trends in motocross, how to invest in the right AI technology, and how AI tools can help riders and teams maintain a long-term competitive advantage.

Emerging AI Trends in Motocross

AI technology is evolving at a rapid pace, and its applications within motocross are expanding. In order to stay ahead, riders and teams must understand the emerging trends and technologies that can provide a competitive edge.

1. AI-Enhanced Performance Analytics

In recent years, AI-enhanced performance analytics have become a significant trend in motocross. These AI systems can analyze an extensive array of data points, such as bike performance, rider movement, track conditions, and even competitor behavior. AI models can then provide real-time insights and long-term performance forecasts.

- **Advanced Data Collection**: Modern AI tools utilize sensors and IoT devices to collect a massive amount of data in real time. Wearables like smart helmets, gloves, and vests can monitor a rider's physiological performance, while sensors on the bike capture critical information such as suspension movement, tire pressure, and engine temperature.
- **Data-Driven Insights**: AI systems can process these data streams to identify patterns, correlations, and anomalies. By understanding how various variables interact, AI can recommend the optimal bike settings for different tracks, the best training methods for the rider, and even suggest improvements in technique.
- **Predictive Analytics**: AI tools are increasingly capable of offering predictive analytics that give teams the foresight to adjust their strategies. For example, AI can forecast a rider's performance under varying conditions, helping teams choose the optimal race plan before the event even begins.

As AI continues to advance, these performance analytics will only become more sophisticated. Teams that invest in these tools early can harness the power of data to fine-tune their approaches and stay ahead of the curve.

2. Real-Time Tracking and Adjustments

Another emerging trend is the use of AI for real-time performance tracking and dynamic adjustments during races. AI can process data on the fly and make immediate recommendations or adjustments to maximize rider performance.

- **In-Race Adjustments**: Real-time data collection allows AI systems to adjust bike settings during the race, such as altering suspension stiffness or adjusting the throttle response to optimize performance based on the current track conditions.
- **Environmental and Track Analysis**: AI tools also analyze environmental factors such as weather, humidity, and track surface conditions. Based on this data, the AI system can recommend specific adjustments to the rider's technique or the bike's settings, allowing them to adapt quickly and stay competitive.
- **Opponent Tracking**: Advanced AI tools can also track competitor performance during the race. By analyzing rivals' movements and lap times, AI can predict their strategy, helping the rider adjust their own approach to maximize chances of success.

With these advancements, AI offers teams the ability to respond to changing conditions and keep a competitive edge by optimizing every aspect of the race in real-time.

3. AI-Driven Virtual Training and Simulation

Virtual training and simulation are becoming vital in developing and refining a rider's skills. AI-powered virtual environments allow riders to simulate races and training sessions, providing them with the opportunity to hone their skills without the risks associated with on-track practice.

- **Simulation Training**: AI simulation tools create realistic virtual environments that mimic the physical conditions of a race. These simulations can include everything from track layout and surface conditions to other riders' movements, offering an accurate reproduction of a real race.

- **Skill Refinement**: Riders can use these simulations to practice specific skills, such as cornering techniques, jump maneuvers, or managing throttle control. AI algorithms analyze their performance and provide instant feedback, helping the rider make quick adjustments and refine their technique in a low-risk setting.
- **Customizable Scenarios**: AI simulations can create customized scenarios based on the rider's weaknesses or specific needs. Whether it's handling aggressive turns or dealing with adverse weather conditions, AI simulations provide targeted training that traditional methods might not cover.

Virtual training environments are an exciting emerging trend that has the potential to significantly accelerate a rider's development while mitigating the risk of injury.

Investing in the Right AI Technology

While AI is transforming motocross, not all AI technologies are created equal. Investing in the right tools can make the difference between maintaining a competitive advantage and falling behind the curve. Here's how riders and teams can identify and invest in the right AI technology to stay ahead of the competition.

1. Understanding the Core Needs of Your Team

Before investing in AI tools, it's crucial to understand the unique needs of your team and your specific racing goals.

- **Assess Your Current Performance**: Start by assessing your team's current performance levels and identifying areas where AI could provide the most value. Do you need to improve rider fitness, bike performance, or race strategy? Understanding these areas will guide your investment decisions.
- **Customization and Scalability**: Consider how customizable and scalable the AI tools are. A good AI system should grow with your team, allowing you to integrate additional features or expand capabilities as your needs evolve. Look for systems that can be tailored to specific aspects of your racing program, such as fitness tracking, bike diagnostics, or track analysis.
- **Consult with Experts**: Many AI companies specialize in motorsports, and consulting with these experts can help you make informed decisions about the most effective tools for your team. Engaging with experienced professionals ensures that you're investing in the right technology for your specific goals.

By understanding your team's unique needs, you can make targeted investments in AI tools that provide the most significant return on investment.

2. Prioritizing AI Systems with Proven ROI

As with any technology investment, it's important to prioritize systems that deliver a proven return on investment (ROI).

- **Performance Metrics**: Look for AI technologies that are backed by data and proven to improve performance. For example, AI-driven wearables and bike sensors can track rider health and bike conditions, improving training efficiency and reducing mechanical issues during races.
- **Long-Term Benefits**: Invest in AI systems that not only provide immediate performance improvements but also offer long-term benefits, such as predictive maintenance tools for the bike, or real-time strategy recommendations during races. These systems offer significant ROI by preventing costly breakdowns and helping you adjust your strategy mid-race.
- **Case Studies and Testimonials**: Research case studies or testimonials from other motocross teams or sports professionals who have successfully used the AI tools you're considering. These real-world examples can provide valuable insights into how the technology has improved performance and delivered results.

Prioritizing AI systems with a demonstrated ROI ensures that your investment pays off both in the short and long term.

3. Embracing Continuous Innovation

AI technology is constantly evolving, and staying ahead of the competition requires a commitment to continuous innovation.

- **Ongoing Updates and Upgrades**: When investing in AI tools, choose systems that offer regular updates and upgrades. This ensures that your technology remains cutting-edge and adapts to new developments in AI research and motocross.
- **Integration with Emerging Technologies**: Keep an eye on how AI integrates with other emerging technologies, such as augmented reality (AR), machine learning, and 5G connectivity. These technologies can further enhance the capabilities of AI tools, enabling even greater performance optimization and predictive power.
- **Research and Development**: Some AI companies focus on developing new technologies that specifically address the needs of motorsports. By partnering with these companies or being early adopters of their solutions, you can stay ahead of the technological curve and ensure that your team always has access to the latest advancements.

Continuous innovation is key to maintaining a long-term competitive advantage. By embracing emerging AI technologies and staying updated on the latest developments, teams can ensure they remain at the forefront of the sport.

Using AI to Maintain Long-Term Competitive Edges

Once a team has adopted AI tools and integrated them into their routine, the challenge becomes maintaining a long-term competitive edge. Here's how AI can be used to ensure that teams continue to stay ahead of the pack:

1. Continuous Monitoring and Optimization

AI systems excel in continuous monitoring and optimization, providing valuable feedback after every training session or race.

- **Longitudinal Data Collection**: By collecting data over time, AI systems can track performance trends, identify recurring issues, and recommend targeted improvements.
- **Adapting to New Challenges**: As riders face new challenges, whether it's different track conditions or evolving racing strategies, AI tools can adapt and recommend solutions based on the data collected over time.

AI's ability to continuously monitor and optimize performance ensures that teams can evolve alongside their competitors and stay ahead of the game.

2. Real-Time Strategy Adaptation

AI can help teams adjust strategies during a race in real time, ensuring they always have a competitive advantage.

- **In-Race Adjustments**: AI can suggest adjustments based on how a rider is performing relative to their competitors, such as recommending different lines or a change in pace.
- **Predicting Opponent Moves**: AI can also anticipate competitors' moves, allowing the rider to adjust their strategy to outmaneuver their rivals.

These real-time adaptations give teams a significant edge, helping them outperform competitors in dynamic race conditions.

3. Keeping Ahead of Competitor Adoption

As AI technology becomes more mainstream, teams need to stay ahead of the curve to maintain their competitive edge.

- **Early Adoption of New Tools**: Teams that adopt new AI tools early have the opportunity to gain a technological advantage before their competitors.
- **Continuous Learning and Improvement**: AI systems learn from every race and training session, offering an ongoing process of improvement. By leveraging these systems, teams can consistently outperform competitors who have not adopted similar tools.

By staying ahead of emerging trends and continuously improving, AI ensures that teams can maintain their competitive advantage over the long term.

Staying ahead in motocross requires more than just raw talent and a well-tuned bike—it requires the strategic use of technology, and AI is one of the most powerful tools in the modern racer's arsenal. By leveraging emerging trends, investing in the right AI technology, and committing to continuous innovation, riders and teams can maintain a long-term competitive edge. AI's ability to analyze data, make real-time adjustments, and predict future outcomes gives teams the insights they need to succeed. By embracing AI tools and staying on the cutting edge, motocross teams can ensure they remain at the forefront of the sport for years to come.

Chapter 6: AI in Event and Race Management

Section 1: Enhancing Event Logistics

In the high-stakes world of professional motocross, the success of an event is often determined by how well the logistics are managed. Race organizers must juggle a multitude of tasks—from scheduling races and managing accommodations to ensuring effective communication with teams and fans. AI is revolutionizing event management by offering innovative solutions that streamline processes, optimize resources, and improve communication. In this section, we'll explore how AI is transforming event logistics, focusing on race schedules and timelines, optimizing rider and team accommodation, and facilitating real-time communication with both teams and fans.

AI for Organizing Race Schedules and Timelines

Race schedules are one of the most complex aspects of event planning in motocross. Organizing multiple races, qualifying heats, and practice sessions while ensuring that everything runs smoothly can be a logistical nightmare. AI is helping streamline this process by providing intelligent scheduling solutions that optimize race timings, minimize downtime, and account for various factors such as track conditions, weather, and rider availability.

1. Automated Scheduling Algorithms

AI-powered scheduling tools are now capable of automating the creation of race schedules based on a variety of inputs, such as the number of participants, race types, and track conditions.

- **Efficient Use of Time**: AI systems can optimize time slots for each race or practice session, ensuring that events proceed smoothly without unnecessary delays. The algorithm can factor in variables like the duration of each race, track preparation time, and the required breaks between sessions.
- **Conflict Resolution**: One of the biggest challenges in organizing a large-scale event is avoiding scheduling conflicts. AI tools can automatically detect potential conflicts, such as overlapping race times or clashes between practice sessions and qualifying rounds, and adjust the schedule accordingly. This ensures that all events are spaced out efficiently without any overlaps.
- **Dynamic Adjustments**: AI systems are not limited to pre-event scheduling; they can also make real-time adjustments during the event. For example, if a race is delayed due to weather or mechanical issues, the AI system can quickly rework the schedule to minimize disruptions. This flexibility ensures that the event stays on track even in the face of unexpected challenges.

With AI's ability to automate, optimize, and adjust race schedules in real-time, organizers can ensure that everything runs smoothly, providing a seamless experience for riders, teams, and spectators alike.

2. Weather and Environmental Considerations

Weather is one of the most unpredictable factors in outdoor sports, and motocross is no exception. Rain, high winds, or extreme temperatures can have a significant impact on the track, the riders' performance, and the race schedule.

- **Real-Time Weather Monitoring**: AI-powered systems can continuously monitor weather conditions using a combination of sensors, satellite data, and weather forecasts. These tools help organizers predict potential weather disruptions and adjust the schedule accordingly.
- **Track Condition Analysis**: AI tools can also assess the impact of weather on track conditions. For example, after rainfall, the system can analyze the track's surface to determine if it's safe to proceed with the race or if it requires maintenance. By integrating weather data and track condition analysis, AI ensures that races proceed under optimal conditions, minimizing risks for riders and maintaining the event's integrity.
- **Predictive Analytics for Delays**: AI can predict when weather conditions will improve, allowing race organizers to make informed decisions about when to resume races. This predictive capability ensures that any delays are minimized, and the event stays on schedule.

By incorporating AI into race scheduling, organizers can ensure that weather disruptions are accounted for, and any necessary changes to the timeline are made efficiently.

Optimizing Rider and Team Accommodation

Accommodating the needs of riders, teams, and staff is a critical part of organizing any large-scale motocross event. From booking hotels and arranging transportation to ensuring that teams have access to the facilities they need, managing accommodations can be a complex task. AI is helping streamline these logistics by optimizing accommodation arrangements based on a variety of factors, ensuring that teams are well-supported throughout the event.

1. Intelligent Accommodation Booking Systems

AI-powered accommodation booking systems can optimize the process of finding hotels and rental properties for riders and team members.

- **Customized Recommendations**: These AI systems take into account the specific preferences of riders and teams, such as proximity to the event venue, hotel amenities, and price range. They can recommend the best accommodations based on these preferences, ensuring a comfortable stay.
- **Dynamic Pricing and Availability**: AI algorithms can monitor availability in real-time and adjust pricing based on demand. By using data from previous events, the system can predict when and where demand will peak, allowing teams to secure the best accommodations at the most cost-effective prices.

- **Group Accommodation Coordination**: For larger teams or staff groups, AI can optimize booking by managing room assignments and ensuring that teams are housed together, making it easier for them to coordinate logistics and reduce travel time.

AI not only simplifies the accommodation process but also ensures that riders and team members are well-supported, allowing them to focus on preparing for the event rather than dealing with logistical headaches.

2. Travel and Transportation Management

AI can also streamline travel logistics by helping teams manage their transportation needs.

- **Optimal Travel Routes**: AI-powered transportation management systems can recommend the most efficient travel routes for riders, teams, and their equipment. These systems consider factors like traffic conditions, road closures, and travel time to ensure that teams arrive at the venue with plenty of time to spare.
- **Flight and Ground Transport Coordination**: AI can assist with booking flights, rental cars, or buses for riders and their teams. The system can synchronize the transportation schedule to ensure that everyone arrives at the event on time, with minimal delays or inconvenience.
- **Transportation Cost Optimization**: AI can also optimize transportation costs by suggesting cost-effective travel options. For example, it may recommend carpooling, group flights, or even shared transport for teams traveling from the same location.

By integrating AI into travel and accommodation management, event organizers can ensure that logistics are streamlined, and teams can focus on what matters most—preparing for the race.

Real-Time Communication with Teams and Fans

Effective communication is critical to the smooth operation of any event, and AI is playing a major role in improving communication between race organizers, teams, and fans. By leveraging AI-powered platforms, event organizers can provide up-to-the-minute updates, improve fan engagement, and ensure that teams have the information they need to make decisions during the race.

1. AI-Driven Communication Platforms for Teams

AI-driven communication platforms allow for seamless, real-time communication between race organizers and teams during the event.

- **Instant Updates**: These platforms can send real-time updates to teams about race delays, track conditions, or schedule changes. AI tools can analyze race data and make suggestions to teams in real time, helping them adjust their strategies accordingly.

- **Coordination Between Staff**: AI-powered communication tools can improve coordination between various team members, including riders, mechanics, and coaches. For example, if there's a mechanical issue during a race, AI tools can alert the mechanic, providing them with detailed diagnostic data to address the issue quickly.
- **Integrated Messaging Systems**: AI messaging systems can integrate with other platforms, such as team apps or social media, allowing race organizers and teams to communicate seamlessly across multiple channels.

Real-time communication ensures that teams are always up-to-date, enabling them to make informed decisions in the heat of the moment.

2. Fan Engagement through AI

AI is also revolutionizing fan engagement by creating more interactive and personalized experiences.

- **Personalized Updates**: AI can send personalized race updates to fans, including live race tracking, notifications of their favorite rider's performance, and real-time standings. By analyzing fans' preferences and behaviors, AI systems can customize communication to make the experience more engaging.
- **Interactive Fan Engagement**: AI-driven chatbots and virtual assistants can engage fans in real-time, answering questions, providing race details, and offering insights into rider performance. These tools help fans stay connected with the event and enhance their overall experience.
- **Social Media Integration**: AI tools can also help automate social media posts, ensuring that fans receive timely updates about race results, schedules, and other important information. AI can analyze social media trends and adjust content to maximize engagement and reach.

By enhancing fan communication and engagement, AI helps boost excitement and ensure that fans feel connected to the event, even from afar.

AI is playing an increasingly crucial role in enhancing the logistics of motocross events. From organizing race schedules and timelines to optimizing accommodations and ensuring real-time communication with teams and fans, AI tools are transforming event management. These technologies offer organizers the ability to streamline processes, improve efficiency, and provide a more engaging experience for both participants and spectators. As AI continues to evolve, its applications in event logistics will only become more sophisticated, offering even greater opportunities to optimize motocross races and create a more seamless, enjoyable event for all involved.

Section 2: Improving Audience Engagement

Motocross events are high-energy, action-packed spectacles that demand the attention and passion of fans. As the sport evolves, so too must the methods of engaging audiences and enhancing their overall experience. In the past, spectators experienced races through traditional broadcasting, while fan engagement was largely passive. However, AI is now reshaping how audiences interact with motocross events, offering enhanced commentary, immersive experiences, and interactive fan communities that create deeper connections between riders, fans, and the sport itself. In this section, we will explore how AI is transforming audience engagement through AI-driven broadcasting and commentary, virtual and augmented reality (VR/AR) experiences, and the creation of interactive fan communities.

AI-Driven Broadcasting and Commentary Enhancements

For years, motocross fans have experienced races through traditional broadcast methods, where commentary is provided by experienced announcers who give insight into the race's progression. While these traditional approaches remain effective, AI-driven broadcasting innovations are revolutionizing the way races are presented to audiences. Through AI technologies, the accuracy, speed, and excitement of commentary and race analysis are enhanced, offering a more engaging viewing experience for fans.

1. Real-Time AI-Powered Commentary

AI-driven commentary tools analyze live race data and provide real-time insights, predictions, and updates that elevate the viewing experience for fans.

- **Instant Data Analysis**: AI can process live data from various sensors on the track and riders, including their speed, lap times, and positioning. Using machine learning algorithms, AI can then analyze this data and offer immediate insights to the audience. For example, AI could predict when a rider is about to overtake another or point out trends in race strategy. By providing these instant insights, AI keeps the audience engaged and informed about the subtleties of the race.
- **Automated Commentators**: AI-powered commentary tools use natural language processing (NLP) to mimic human commentary. These systems are able to create seamless, articulate narration based on real-time race data, ensuring that fans receive timely, accurate updates on the race without requiring manual intervention. This reduces the risk of human error and allows for more consistent, fluid commentary.
- **Contextual Race Insights**: AI tools can also go beyond basic race statistics by providing in-depth analysis. For instance, AI can assess the impact of track conditions, rider performance, and weather on the race, offering fans a deeper understanding of why certain events are happening. This contextual commentary adds richness to the viewing experience, enhancing the level of engagement.

With these AI-powered commentary enhancements, fans are not just watching a race—they are gaining a deeper understanding of the strategic elements, performance metrics, and competitive dynamics that shape the sport.

2. Personalized Viewing Experience

AI is also enhancing the way fans interact with broadcasts by offering personalized viewing experiences.

- **Tailored Content**: AI systems can analyze fan preferences and viewing history to create a personalized race experience. For example, if a fan regularly follows a specific rider, AI can prioritize that rider's race data and offer additional insights into their performance throughout the event. AI can also curate highlight reels based on individual fan interests, ensuring that viewers get the most relevant content tailored to their tastes.
- **Smart Highlights**: AI-driven systems are able to automatically identify key moments in a race, such as crashes, overtakes, and other significant events. Fans can view these highlights in real-time, often within seconds of the event occurring, giving them a more interactive and immersive experience. This means that viewers can feel more connected to the action, even when they aren't watching every moment live.
- **Voice-Controlled Interactions**: AI technology, integrated with voice-command systems like Amazon Alexa or Google Assistant, allows fans to interact with the race broadcast using voice commands. Fans can ask questions about a rider's statistics, track conditions, or race progress, and the AI-powered system will provide accurate, immediate answers. This provides a more dynamic, user-controlled experience that engages the viewer throughout the race.

By using AI to personalize the viewing experience, broadcasts become more immersive, allowing fans to dive deeper into the action and feel more connected to the race.

Virtual and Augmented Reality Experiences for Fans

Virtual and augmented reality are becoming powerful tools for increasing fan engagement, offering fans an immersive experience that makes them feel as though they are part of the action. AI plays a crucial role in enhancing VR and AR experiences, offering new and exciting ways for fans to interact with races, riders, and the sport itself.

1. Immersive Virtual Reality Experiences

AI-driven VR experiences are pushing the boundaries of fan engagement by creating fully immersive simulations of motocross events.

- **Live Race Simulation**: AI can be used to create VR simulations that allow fans to experience a motocross race from a first-person perspective. Fans can view the race from the point of view of their favorite rider, experiencing the thrills, challenges, and adrenaline of the race. By integrating real-time race data, these VR experiences can be as close to the actual race as possible, giving fans an authentic sense of being in the race themselves.

- **Virtual Track Tours**: AI-driven VR experiences can also give fans access to virtual tours of tracks, letting them explore the racing environment in detail. Fans can zoom in on specific parts of the track, view detailed terrain analysis, and learn about the history of each race location. This type of immersive content helps fans develop a deeper understanding of the sport's intricacies while enhancing their connection to the event.
- **Interactive Race Training**: AI-powered VR systems can even let fans participate in virtual training sessions, where they can experience what it's like to train and compete as a motocross rider. Through gamified VR experiences, fans can practice maneuvers, adjust bike settings, and compete against other virtual racers, providing an entirely new way to engage with the sport.

By immersing fans in these AI-driven VR experiences, motocross events become more than just something to watch—they become an adventure fans can participate in themselves.

2. Augmented Reality for Enhanced Fan Interaction

While VR offers an immersive, standalone experience, augmented reality (AR) enhances the real-world experience by adding virtual elements to a live race.

- **On-Track AR Displays**: AI-powered AR systems can overlay real-time data on the live race through fans' smartphones or AR glasses. For example, as a fan watches a race in person, they could view live lap times, rider statistics, and even predictive race insights displayed over the track in their view. This information provides fans with a richer, more engaging experience, allowing them to track the race's progress in real-time.
- **AR-Enhanced Merchandise**: AI-driven AR tools can also enhance the fan shopping experience. For example, by scanning merchandise with their smartphone, fans can view 3D models of bikes, gear, or other memorabilia. They could even unlock exclusive content like interviews or behind-the-scenes footage, adding an extra layer of engagement.
- **Interactive Fan Experiences**: During race breaks or intermissions, AI-driven AR games can be used to engage fans in the stands. Whether it's a virtual scavenger hunt, a trivia contest, or an interactive leaderboard game, AR tools allow fans to stay engaged during downtime while deepening their connection to the event.

AI-powered AR experiences not only enhance the in-person event but also transform the way fans interact with the sport and its ecosystem.

Using AI to Build Interactive Fan Communities

Beyond improving individual experiences, AI is also helping to build and foster fan communities that allow fans to interact with each other, share content, and engage with the sport on a deeper level. Through AI-driven platforms, fans can become part of a larger, interconnected motocross community that keeps them engaged year-round.

1. AI-Powered Social Platforms

AI is transforming the way fans interact with each other by providing personalized, intelligent social platforms that encourage engagement.

- **Content Personalization**: AI can track user behavior on social platforms and deliver personalized content based on their interests. Whether a fan is into particular riders, specific teams, or historical race stats, AI can curate content that keeps them coming back for more.
- **Fan Interaction Tools**: AI-driven chatbots and virtual assistants help fans interact with the community and get answers to their questions instantly. These tools can direct fans to specific content, connect them with others who share similar interests, or provide real-time race insights and updates.
- **Fan-Generated Content Curation**: AI can also help fans share and promote their own content. By analyzing trends and patterns in fan posts, AI can recommend fan-generated content for wider distribution, creating opportunities for fans to get their voices heard and feel more connected to the broader community.

By fostering an AI-enhanced social environment, fans can build connections with each other and stay more deeply engaged with motocross, turning their love of the sport into a year-round passion.

2. AI-Driven Event Engagement

AI tools can also drive fan engagement during live events by encouraging participation and creating memorable experiences.

- **Live Polls and Contests**: Fans can use AI-powered platforms to participate in live polls, contests, and interactive games. Whether voting on race predictions, answering trivia questions, or engaging in challenges, fans stay involved and connected with the event as it unfolds.
- **Fan Feedback Systems**: AI systems can gather real-time feedback from fans during the race, allowing organizers to adjust the event experience based on audience preferences. For example, if fans express a desire for more information on a particular rider or track, AI can automatically adjust the broadcast to meet this demand.
- **Post-Event Engagement**: After the race, AI can help maintain engagement by delivering personalized highlights, behind-the-scenes content, and exclusive interviews. These post-event interactions keep the conversation going long after the race ends, ensuring that fans stay connected and continue to engage with the sport.

AI-powered event engagement tools offer fans new ways to participate in the sport and feel like active contributors to the motocross community.

AI is transforming the way motocross engages with its audience, creating deeper, more immersive experiences for fans. By enhancing broadcasting and commentary, introducing VR and AR technologies, and building interactive fan communities, AI is revolutionizing the way fans connect with the sport. These innovations not only enrich the viewing experience but also foster stronger relationships between fans, riders, and the broader motocross ecosystem. As AI technology continues to evolve, the future of fan engagement in motocross looks brighter than ever, promising more dynamic, interactive, and personalized experiences that will keep fans coming back for more.

Section 3: Sustainability and Ethics in AI-Powered Events

As AI continues to revolutionize the way motocross events are managed, it brings with it a host of new opportunities, not just for performance optimization and fan engagement, but also for sustainability and ethical considerations. The environmental footprint of large-scale events and the ethical implications of AI-powered decision-making are becoming important aspects that require careful consideration. In this section, we will explore how AI can help reduce the environmental impact of motocross events, the ethical issues surrounding AI usage, and the need for proper regulation to ensure fair competition.

Reducing Environmental Impact with AI

Motocross, like many motorsport disciplines, carries a significant environmental footprint. From the energy consumed by transport logistics to the resources required for building and maintaining racing tracks, the ecological impact is considerable. However, AI has the potential to help mitigate these environmental effects, making motocross events more sustainable without compromising their exciting nature.

1. Optimizing Transport and Logistics

Transporting equipment, bikes, and teams to and from race locations is one of the largest contributors to the environmental footprint of a motocross event. AI can streamline transportation logistics, reducing unnecessary travel and emissions.

- **Route Optimization**: AI-powered logistics platforms can plan the most efficient routes for transportation. By factoring in variables such as traffic, fuel consumption, and road conditions, AI can minimize the amount of fuel used, thereby reducing carbon emissions. Additionally, AI tools can adjust travel plans in real time to account for changes in weather, delays, or other disruptions, further optimizing the transportation process.
- **Carbon Footprint Tracking**: AI can also track and analyze the carbon footprint of events in real time, offering insights into areas where emissions can be reduced. For example, AI could recommend switching to electric-powered vehicles for transport or suggest carpooling or public transport for teams and staff to minimize the number of vehicles used. By tracking data on fuel consumption and emissions, AI helps teams and organizers make data-driven decisions to reduce their environmental impact.

By optimizing transport logistics and tracking the carbon footprint of events, AI can help reduce the environmental burden of motocross, contributing to a more sustainable future for the sport.

2. Energy Consumption Management

Large-scale events like motocross races consume considerable amounts of energy for lighting, sound systems, cooling, and other infrastructure needs. AI can help reduce energy consumption by intelligently managing these systems.

- **Smart Energy Grids**: AI can monitor and control the distribution of energy throughout the event, optimizing the use of electricity and ensuring that energy is only used when necessary. For instance, AI can dim lights or turn off non-essential equipment during low-traffic periods, reducing overall consumption.
- **Renewable Energy Integration**: AI can also facilitate the integration of renewable energy sources, such as solar or wind power, into the energy supply of the event. By monitoring weather patterns and energy demand, AI can intelligently decide when to draw power from renewable sources, ensuring that the event runs as sustainably as possible.
- **Real-Time Efficiency Adjustments**: AI-powered systems can monitor energy consumption in real-time and adjust settings to maximize energy efficiency. For example, AI can regulate the temperature of cooling systems based on current weather conditions, adjusting to avoid excessive energy use during cooler periods.

With AI helping to optimize energy usage, motocross events can become significantly more energy-efficient, contributing to sustainability efforts and reducing the environmental impact of the sport.

3. Waste Reduction and Resource Efficiency

Another key area where AI can help improve sustainability in motocross events is in reducing waste and promoting resource efficiency.

- **Waste Management Systems**: AI-powered waste management systems can track waste production throughout an event and optimize disposal strategies. These systems can identify patterns in waste generation, such as high volumes of packaging materials or plastic bottles, and suggest more sustainable alternatives, such as using recyclable or biodegradable materials.
- **Resource Allocation**: AI can also help optimize the use of materials, such as track construction supplies, food and beverage containers, and even merchandise. By predicting demand and minimizing overproduction, AI ensures that resources are used efficiently, reducing waste and promoting sustainable practices.
- **Circular Economy Approaches**: AI can help implement circular economy principles, ensuring that materials and resources used in motocross events are recycled or reused rather than disposed of. AI systems can track the life cycle of materials used during the event, ensuring they are returned to the supply chain for reuse, further reducing waste and promoting sustainability.

Through AI-powered waste and resource management, motocross events can reduce their environmental impact while promoting more sustainable practices in the industry.

Ethical Considerations in AI Usage

While the benefits of AI in motocross are undeniable, its use also raises important ethical considerations. As AI systems become more integrated into the management of races, training, and fan engagement, it's crucial to examine how these technologies are used and ensure they are being applied ethically and responsibly.

1. Data Privacy and Security

AI systems in motocross rely on vast amounts of data, including rider statistics, bike performance, fan interactions, and environmental factors. Protecting this data and ensuring its ethical use is one of the most important ethical concerns in AI adoption.

- **Rider and Fan Privacy**: With wearable devices and sensors tracking riders' biometrics, AI systems collect sensitive data that can provide insights into a rider's health, fatigue, and performance. This data must be handled securely to protect the privacy of the riders. Similarly, fan data collected through AI-driven platforms must be safeguarded to ensure that individuals' personal information is not misused.
- **Data Ownership**: Clear guidelines must be established regarding who owns the data collected by AI systems. Should the riders, teams, or event organizers have ownership of the data, or should it be available to third-party companies who provide AI tools? Ethical considerations must be made to ensure that data is used transparently and for the benefit of the sport, rather than for exploitation.
- **Bias in AI Algorithms**: AI systems are only as good as the data they are trained on. If the data fed into AI algorithms is biased, the output can be skewed in ways that perpetuate existing inequalities. For example, if certain riders or teams are underrepresented in the data, AI predictions could be biased, potentially disadvantaging those riders. Ensuring fairness in the way data is collected and processed is crucial to maintaining an ethical standard in AI-powered systems.

Ensuring the ethical handling of data, maintaining privacy, and addressing algorithmic biases are crucial components of AI integration into motocross.

2. AI and Rider Autonomy

AI can offer powerful tools for training, performance analysis, and race strategy. However, it's essential to balance the use of AI with rider autonomy. Riders should not feel that their performance or strategy is entirely dictated by AI systems.

- **Maintaining Human Agency**: While AI can provide valuable insights and recommendations, it's important that riders and teams retain the ability to make decisions based on their own judgment, experience, and instincts. Overreliance on AI could stifle creativity and intuition, which are critical components of successful racing.
- **AI as a Supplement, Not a Replacement**: AI should be viewed as a tool to enhance, rather than replace, the human aspects of motocross. Riders must have the autonomy to choose how to use AI suggestions, ensuring that they remain in control of their racing decisions.

Balancing the influence of AI with human decision-making ensures that riders' skills, instincts, and individuality continue to play a central role in the sport.

Ensuring Fair Competition Through AI Regulation

As AI becomes more integrated into the motocross world, ensuring fair competition is critical. AI-driven performance enhancements, race strategy optimizations, and real-time insights can give certain riders or teams a competitive edge. To maintain fairness, clear regulations must be put in place to govern the use of AI in racing.

1. AI Regulation in Equipment and Performance Enhancement

AI tools that optimize bike settings, track analysis, and rider performance could create a situation where only the teams with access to the best AI tools have a competitive advantage. To ensure fair competition, governing bodies must regulate the use of AI-powered performance enhancements.

- **Standardized Equipment**: Rules must be implemented to ensure that all teams have access to the same types of AI tools and equipment. This prevents a situation where certain teams could benefit from more advanced or exclusive AI technology, creating an uneven playing field.
- **Monitoring AI-Driven Adjustments**: AI can help teams adjust bike settings, engine power, and suspension based on real-time data. Regulations should be put in place to ensure that AI-driven adjustments are within fair limits, preventing teams from gaining an unfair advantage through technology alone.

By regulating the use of AI-driven performance enhancements, motocross can maintain a level playing field where riders' skills, not just technology, determine the outcome of races.

2. Transparency in AI Decision-Making

The algorithms and models used in AI systems must be transparent and understandable to all stakeholders, including riders, teams, and fans.

- **Open AI Systems**: Regulations should require that AI systems used in racing are open and transparent. This ensures that riders and teams understand how AI makes decisions, which in turn helps to prevent manipulations or biases in performance analysis and strategy recommendations.
- **Third-Party Auditing**: To ensure fairness and transparency, independent third parties could be tasked with auditing AI systems used in racing. These audits would verify that AI systems are functioning as intended and that no unfair advantages are being gained through manipulation or unethical use of the technology.

With proper regulation and oversight, AI can be integrated into motocross in a way that enhances competition without compromising fairness or transparency.

While AI presents incredible opportunities to enhance motocross events, it also raises significant challenges related to sustainability and ethics. From reducing environmental impact through optimized logistics and energy management to ensuring the ethical use of data and AI tools, the future of AI in motocross will require careful thought and regulation. By focusing on sustainability and fairness, and by ensuring that AI enhances rather than replaces human skill, the motocross community can fully embrace the potential of AI while maintaining the integrity of the sport.

Chapter 7: The Role of AI in Rider Safety and Injury Recovery

Section 1: AI for Preventing Injuries

Motocross, one of the most physically demanding and high-risk sports, presents significant challenges to rider safety. The high-speed nature of the sport, combined with rough terrain, jumps, and intense physical exertion, increases the likelihood of accidents and injuries. However, advancements in technology, particularly in artificial intelligence (AI), are revolutionizing the way the sport approaches safety. By providing real-time data and predictive insights, AI tools are being integrated into training, racing, and injury prevention protocols to protect riders and help them recover more effectively. In this section, we will explore the role AI plays in preventing injuries by monitoring rider fatigue, issuing alerts for dangerous conditions, and offering adaptive coaching strategies to minimize risk.

Monitoring Rider Fatigue with Wearable Tech

One of the most critical factors in preventing motocross injuries is managing rider fatigue. As a physically demanding sport, motocross requires extreme endurance and mental focus. Fatigue, whether physical or mental, significantly increases the risk of accidents, as tired riders are more likely to make errors in judgment, lose control, or miscalculate obstacles. AI-driven wearable technology plays a pivotal role in monitoring fatigue and providing real-time data to help prevent injuries.

1. Wearable Devices for Tracking Physiological Metrics

Wearables are devices that riders wear during training or races to collect physiological data. These devices can measure a wide range of metrics, including heart rate, body temperature, muscle strain, and movement patterns. By tracking these metrics, AI systems can analyze how a rider's body is responding to the stress of racing or training.

- **Heart Rate and Recovery**: Wearable devices can track heart rate variability, which is a key indicator of fatigue and recovery. When a rider's heart rate does not return to baseline levels after exertion, it can signal overtraining or the onset of fatigue. AI algorithms analyze this data to determine when a rider is at risk of burnout or physical strain, providing early warnings about potential fatigue-related injuries.
- **Muscle Strain and Recovery**: AI-powered wearables can also monitor muscle strain and track physical exertion levels, helping coaches and riders understand when they are pushing their limits. Excessive strain on muscles or joints can lead to long-term injuries, such as sprains, strains, or stress fractures. By using AI to detect signs of overexertion, riders can adjust their training or racing intensity to avoid injury.
- **Movement Efficiency**: AI-powered wearables can assess the efficiency of a rider's movements by monitoring body position, posture, and the way they handle the bike. Poor technique or inefficient movements can place undue strain on the rider's body,

leading to fatigue and injury. These wearables give coaches insights into how a rider's technique might be causing unnecessary fatigue, allowing them to adjust training techniques and improve safety.

By continuously monitoring these key metrics, AI-powered wearable technology helps riders and coaches identify the early signs of fatigue, enabling proactive measures to prevent injuries before they occur.

2. Real-Time Fatigue Alerts

AI systems can provide real-time alerts when a rider's physiological data suggests they are reaching critical fatigue levels. These alerts can be sent directly to the rider, their coach, or team, helping them make timely decisions to reduce the risk of injury.

- **Fatigue Thresholds**: AI systems can be programmed with individual rider thresholds for fatigue, based on their historical data and performance. When the system detects that the rider is approaching or surpassing these thresholds, it triggers an alert, prompting the rider to reduce their intensity, take a break, or adjust their strategy.
- **Mental Fatigue Detection**: Mental fatigue is just as dangerous as physical exhaustion. AI systems can track indicators of cognitive strain, such as reaction time and decision-making patterns. Slower reaction times or erratic behavior on the track can be signs of mental fatigue. AI can help detect these patterns and warn riders or coaches to take preventive actions to avoid mistakes or accidents.
- **AI-Driven Monitoring During Races**: During races, where fatigue is most likely to set in, AI systems continue to monitor a rider's condition in real-time. With live alerts, teams can provide feedback to riders, encouraging them to adjust their pacing or even rest, if necessary, during pit stops.

By leveraging real-time data and fatigue alerts, AI systems help mitigate the risks associated with fatigue, keeping riders safe and reducing their chances of sustaining an injury during both training and competition.

AI Alerts for Dangerous Riding Conditions

In addition to monitoring rider fatigue, AI systems can also detect dangerous environmental conditions that could put riders at risk. Motocross tracks are dynamic and ever-changing, with conditions varying due to weather, terrain, and track wear. AI-powered systems can predict and identify these hazards in real-time, offering valuable insights that can help prevent accidents before they occur.

1. Weather and Track Condition Prediction

Weather conditions, such as rain or extreme heat, can dramatically alter the safety of a motocross track. AI systems are capable of analyzing weather forecasts, real-time weather data, and track conditions to predict potential risks.

- **Rain and Wet Conditions**: Wet tracks significantly increase the likelihood of crashes, as mud and slippery surfaces can reduce traction. AI systems can integrate with weather data to predict rainfall and adjust track conditions accordingly. By monitoring precipitation levels and surface moisture, AI can provide warnings about potential hazards, allowing riders to adjust their speed or racing technique.
- **Heat and Exhaustion**: Extreme heat can cause dehydration and overheating, which in turn can lead to fatigue and decreased performance. AI tools can track environmental data, such as temperature and humidity, and compare them with a rider's physiological data to predict when a rider may be at risk of heat stress.
- **Track Surface Wear and Tear**: As races progress, the track surface changes due to the combined impact of the riders and the natural terrain. AI systems equipped with sensors can monitor track conditions, identifying worn-down areas or increasing levels of risk due to bumps, loose dirt, or sharp turns. This allows race organizers to make adjustments or provide warnings to riders about potential hazards, improving overall safety.

By predicting dangerous track conditions based on weather and terrain data, AI systems enhance rider awareness and reduce the likelihood of injuries caused by environmental factors.

2. Predicting and Preventing Crashes

AI-powered systems can also detect patterns in rider behavior that may lead to accidents. By analyzing historical crash data and rider performance, AI can predict when a rider may be in danger of making a critical mistake.

- **Riding Patterns and Risk Indicators**: AI systems can track a rider's behavior during practice sessions and races. For example, if a rider consistently approaches a corner too quickly or fails to adjust their speed appropriately for certain jumps, AI can alert them to their risky behavior. By recognizing these patterns, AI provides warnings before a crash occurs.
- **Crash Prediction Models**: AI uses machine learning to analyze crash data and identify the conditions under which accidents are most likely to occur. For example, by analyzing factors such as speed, body posture, and the position of the rider relative to obstacles, AI systems can predict potential crashes. These predictions can lead to automatic system alerts, allowing riders and their teams to take preventive actions.
- **Real-Time Alerts During Races**: AI can also integrate with communication systems to issue real-time crash alerts to riders. For instance, if a rider is about to approach a high-risk section of the track, AI can deliver a warning via an earpiece, advising them to slow down or adjust their posture to avoid a crash.

By predicting and preventing crashes through AI-powered crash prediction models and real-time alerts, the likelihood of injury is significantly reduced, enabling a safer racing environment for all participants.

Adaptive Coaching for Minimizing Risk

AI also plays a crucial role in adaptive coaching, which focuses on adjusting training programs and techniques to minimize the risk of injury. Coaches can use AI tools to track a rider's progress, detect signs of overtraining or fatigue, and adapt their training sessions accordingly.

1. Customized Training Programs

AI helps coaches create customized training programs based on a rider's unique needs, strengths, and weaknesses. By analyzing data from wearables and performance trackers, AI identifies areas where riders may be at risk of injury, such as poor technique, muscle imbalances, or excessive strain.

- **Biomechanical Feedback**: AI can provide biomechanical feedback on a rider's technique, offering insights into body posture, bike handling, and movement efficiency. If a rider's technique is contributing to injury risk, AI will suggest adjustments to reduce strain on the body.
- **Load Management**: Overtraining is a common cause of injuries in motocross. AI systems can monitor workload and training intensity, providing alerts when a rider is pushing too hard without adequate rest. This helps avoid overuse injuries, such as tendinitis or stress fractures, and ensures that riders are training safely.

2. AI-Driven Injury Prevention Exercises

AI can also recommend specific exercises to improve strength, flexibility, and mobility, helping riders build resilience against injury. By analyzing data on a rider's movements and muscle weaknesses, AI can suggest exercises that target vulnerable areas.

- **Strengthening Weak Areas**: If AI detects imbalances in muscle strength or joint stability, it can suggest exercises that target those areas to improve overall strength and reduce the risk of injury.
- **Preventative Rehabilitation**: AI can track a rider's recovery from past injuries and suggest rehabilitation exercises to minimize the chances of re-injury.

Through adaptive coaching strategies, AI ensures that riders are always training in a way that minimizes injury risk, optimizing their performance while keeping them safe.

The integration of AI into injury prevention in motocross is transforming the way riders train, race, and recover. By utilizing wearable tech to monitor fatigue, issuing alerts for dangerous conditions, and offering adaptive coaching strategies, AI helps riders avoid injuries and stay safe on the track. With the potential to predict and prevent accidents, manage physical strain, and adapt training programs to individual needs, AI is proving to be an invaluable tool in enhancing rider safety and promoting longevity in the sport. As technology continues to advance, AI will undoubtedly play an even more significant role in making motocross a safer and more sustainable sport for all involved.

Section 2: Accelerating Injury Recovery

Injuries in motocross are not just physical setbacks but also emotional and mental challenges for riders. When a rider is sidelined by an injury, the path to recovery becomes just as important as the path to victory. In traditional sports, recovery often depended on a combination of physical therapy, rest, and coaching, but with the advent of artificial intelligence (AI), recovery processes have become faster, more accurate, and data-driven. AI technology is now playing a significant role in accelerating injury recovery, offering personalized rehabilitation programs, tracking progress in real time, and providing virtual coaching that keeps riders motivated throughout their recovery journey. This section will explore how AI is reshaping the way injuries are treated and recovery is managed in motocross, offering solutions that not only help riders heal but also ensure they return to the track in peak condition.

AI-Assisted Physical Therapy Programs

Physical therapy is a cornerstone of injury recovery, helping athletes regain strength, mobility, and functionality. Traditionally, therapy programs were designed based on the therapist's experience and generalized guidelines, but AI technology has introduced a more tailored and adaptive approach to rehabilitation. AI-assisted physical therapy programs use data-driven insights and machine learning to create personalized recovery plans for each rider.

1. Customizing Rehabilitation Plans Based on Rider's Needs

The process of AI-assisted physical therapy begins with a comprehensive analysis of the rider's injury, physical capabilities, and previous performance data. Wearables, motion-capture devices, and sensors can track the rider's movement patterns, muscle strength, joint mobility, and other physiological parameters. AI systems process this data to identify imbalances, weaknesses, and areas that need strengthening. Based on this analysis, a customized rehabilitation plan is developed.

- **Personalized Recovery Protocols**: AI analyzes the severity and type of injury to determine the appropriate rehabilitation exercises and activities that will best support the rider's recovery. These protocols evolve as the rider progresses through their recovery journey, adjusting based on real-time feedback. For example, if a rider is recovering from a knee injury, AI can suggest exercises that gradually build strength around the knee joint while limiting the risk of overexertion.
- **Targeted Rehabilitation**: AI can use biomechanical data to target specific muscles or joints that need more attention. For example, if a rider's hip flexors have become weak after a leg injury, AI can create an exercise regimen designed to improve flexibility and strength in those areas. By focusing on the individual's weaknesses, AI enhances the effectiveness of rehabilitation.

2. Monitoring Rehabilitation in Real Time

One of the key advantages of AI in rehabilitation is its ability to provide real-time data on the rider's progress. As riders engage in rehabilitation exercises, AI systems continually monitor their movements, capturing data on muscle activation, joint angles, and range of motion.

- **Real-Time Feedback**: AI-driven rehabilitation platforms provide immediate feedback on exercise performance. For example, if a rider performs an exercise incorrectly or does not reach the correct range of motion, the AI can alert the rider to adjust their technique. This immediate correction helps prevent compensatory movements, which could lead to further injuries.
- **Tracking Progress Over Time**: With AI, progress isn't just measured through subjective self-reports or occasional check-ups. Continuous data collection during every session provides a detailed picture of the rider's recovery journey. AI can analyze trends in improvement, pinpoint areas that are not progressing as expected, and adjust the rehabilitation plan accordingly. For instance, if the rider's mobility is improving more slowly than anticipated, the AI might recommend an increase in stretching or a different form of exercise.

3. Preventing Re-Injury and Optimizing Recovery Pace

AI-assisted rehabilitation can prevent re-injury by ensuring the rider does not return to training or racing too soon. AI analyzes the rider's physiological data to determine when it's safe to increase activity levels or return to the track.

- **Injury Risk Prediction**: By tracking real-time progress and integrating historical injury data, AI systems can predict when a rider might be at risk of re-injury. If the system detects that a particular muscle group has not regained full strength or that joint mobility is still limited, it can advise caution.
- **Adjusting Recovery Pace**: One of the challenges of rehabilitation is determining the right pace. If a rider rushes back into training too soon, they risk exacerbating the injury. AI systems can track metrics like muscle endurance, flexibility, and joint health to determine when a rider is ready for more intense physical activities. By adjusting the pace of recovery to match the rider's physiological state, AI reduces the likelihood of re-injury.

Through these personalized, data-driven rehabilitation programs, AI assists riders in recovering more efficiently and safely, offering a level of precision and adaptability that was previously unattainable in traditional therapy settings.

Tracking Rehabilitation Progress with Data

AI's ability to collect, analyze, and interpret vast amounts of data is crucial for tracking rehabilitation progress. Unlike traditional recovery methods that rely heavily on subjective feedback, AI provides objective, data-driven insights into how well the rider is healing and whether the rehabilitation plan is effective.

1. Collecting Comprehensive Data on Recovery Metrics

AI systems are designed to collect an array of data points that provide a holistic view of a rider's recovery process. This data can be gathered through various methods, including wearables, motion sensors, and biomechanics tools. Some key metrics include:

- **Movement Range and Joint Health**: AI tracks the rider's range of motion in the injured area and compares it with baseline data, noting improvements or stagnation. This data helps determine if the rider's joints are healing properly or if further rehabilitation is needed.
- **Muscle Activation and Strength**: AI monitors muscle strength and activation patterns, ensuring that the rider is regaining muscle function in a balanced way. If certain muscles are underperforming, AI can recommend exercises specifically designed to target those muscles.
- **Pain and Fatigue Levels**: Data from wearables can be used to track pain levels and fatigue. The AI system takes this information into account when adjusting the recovery protocol, ensuring that riders aren't pushing through pain or fatigue, which could prolong recovery or cause reinjury.

These metrics are tracked over time, giving both the rider and medical professionals an in-depth understanding of the rider's recovery status. By continuously collecting data, AI systems can identify trends and highlight areas of concern before they become serious issues.

2. Using AI for Predictive Recovery Modeling

AI doesn't just track recovery; it also predicts future recovery trends based on the data collected. By analyzing the rider's progress, AI can create predictive models that forecast the timeline for full recovery.

- **Forecasting Recovery Timelines**: AI models analyze patterns from thousands of similar injuries and recovery cases to predict how long a rider's recovery might take. This helps set realistic expectations for the rider and their team and allows for better planning regarding when the rider can return to racing.
- **Personalized Predictions**: Unlike generalized predictions based on a broad population, AI tailors these recovery timelines to the individual's unique data, accounting for factors like their age, fitness level, injury type, and response to treatment. This personalized approach enhances recovery planning and can help reduce the psychological stress of the recovery process.

3. Sharing Data with Medical Professionals

AI systems also facilitate better communication between the rider and their medical team by providing real-time access to recovery data. The rider's progress can be monitored remotely, allowing doctors, physiotherapists, and coaches to make informed decisions about treatment plans.

- **Remote Monitoring and Consultation**: Through cloud-based platforms, the rider's rehabilitation data can be shared with multiple medical professionals in real time.

This enables faster decision-making and allows for consultations with specialists if needed, ensuring that the recovery plan is always in alignment with the latest medical insights.

- **Data-Driven Adjustments**: When medical professionals access the AI-generated data, they can make adjustments to the rider's rehabilitation plan. If a particular treatment method isn't working as expected, AI can help professionals evaluate alternative approaches based on data-driven insights.

By using data to track rehabilitation progress, AI ensures that riders' recovery is not left to guesswork. It provides a level of accuracy and insight that supports timely interventions and promotes optimal healing.

Virtual Coaches for Recovery Motivation

In addition to physical rehabilitation, the mental and emotional aspects of recovery are equally crucial for a rider's return to full health. The road to recovery can be long and frustrating, with many riders struggling to stay motivated. AI-powered virtual coaching tools are helping to bridge this gap by offering personalized, consistent, and motivational support throughout the recovery process.

1. Motivating Through Progress Tracking

Virtual coaches use AI to track a rider's progress and keep them motivated by showing tangible results. Through wearable technology and other data collection methods, AI generates weekly or daily reports on how much the rider has improved.

- **Positive Reinforcement**: Virtual coaches offer positive reinforcement by recognizing milestones in recovery, such as regaining full range of motion or increasing strength in a specific muscle group.
- **Visual Progress Tracking**: AI-driven platforms may provide visual progress reports, showing graphs or charts that compare the rider's current status with their pre-injury baseline. These visual cues help keep the rider focused and motivated to continue their rehabilitation efforts.

2. Goal Setting and Achievements

AI can help riders set realistic recovery goals, breaking down the rehabilitation process into smaller, achievable milestones. These micro-goals might include small improvements in muscle strength, flexibility, or performance on specific rehabilitation exercises. Virtual coaches keep riders on track by adjusting goals as progress is made.

- **Adjustable Goals**: Based on the rider's progress, AI can update goals dynamically, ensuring that the rider is always challenged but not overwhelmed.
- **Gamification of Recovery**: Virtual coaches can incorporate gamified elements into the recovery process, making rehabilitation more engaging. Riders might earn points or rewards for achieving specific goals, adding an element of fun and competition to the recovery journey.

3. Emotional Support and Encouragement

Virtual coaches also play an important role in providing emotional support. Riders may experience frustration, self-doubt, or anxiety during their recovery, and AI-powered coaches can offer encouragement and motivation. Through conversational AI, these virtual coaches can provide positive affirmations and empathetic responses that help riders maintain a positive mindset.

In conclusion, AI is revolutionizing injury recovery in motocross by offering personalized rehabilitation programs, monitoring progress with real-time data, and providing virtual coaching that motivates and supports riders. This technological revolution is not only helping riders heal faster but also ensuring that they return to the track stronger and more resilient than before. By enhancing recovery through AI, motocross athletes can maintain peak performance levels and continue to push the limits

Section 3: Mental Health Support with AI

Motocross racing is one of the most physically demanding and high-risk sports, but its emotional and mental toll is often overlooked. Riders are not only dealing with physical injuries but also the psychological strain that comes with intense competition, the pressure to perform, the fear of injury, and the uncertainty of recovery. Mental health challenges, such as stress, anxiety, and depression, are just as prevalent among athletes as physical injuries, and motocross riders are no exception. Fortunately, artificial intelligence (AI) is emerging as a crucial tool in addressing mental health concerns within the sport. By identifying stress levels through biometrics, offering tools to reduce anxiety and improve focus, and providing long-term mental wellness planning, AI is empowering riders to maintain not only their physical health but their mental well-being too.

This section will delve into how AI technologies are enhancing the mental health support available to motocross riders, providing personalized interventions and promoting long-term emotional resilience in a sport that demands peak mental performance.

Identifying Stress Levels Through Biometrics

Stress management is a key component of mental health, particularly in high-stakes environments like motocross. Whether it's the pressure of competition, fear of injury, or the overwhelming drive to perform, riders often face mental hurdles that can impact their concentration, performance, and overall well-being. AI technologies have the ability to detect early signs of stress, providing real-time monitoring and interventions that can help riders manage their mental state.

1. Monitoring Physiological Stress Indicators

Wearable devices embedded with AI-driven sensors can monitor physiological stress indicators such as heart rate variability (HRV), sweat levels, skin temperature, and breathing patterns. These biometrics offer real-time data on a rider's emotional and physical stress responses, providing a window into how stress is affecting their body.

- **Heart Rate Variability (HRV)**: HRV is a critical indicator of stress and recovery, as it reflects the balance between the sympathetic nervous system (fight or flight) and parasympathetic nervous system (rest and digest). A lower HRV often indicates higher stress levels, while a higher HRV suggests a more balanced mental state. AI algorithms can analyze HRV trends and alert riders to potentially harmful stress patterns.
- **Sweat and Skin Temperature**: Stress can trigger changes in sweat production and skin temperature. Wearables that monitor these factors can provide real-time insights into how the rider is coping with stress. When AI identifies patterns of excessive sweating or elevated skin temperature, it can suggest strategies for calming the body and mind, such as breathing exercises or brief rest periods.
- **Breathing Patterns**: Breathing rates and patterns can be used to gauge stress levels. Rapid, shallow breathing is often associated with anxiety and stress, while slow, deep breaths signal a relaxed state. AI-driven tools can analyze breathing patterns during both training and competition, identifying moments when stress levels are peaking and recommending techniques to regain control.

Through continuous monitoring of these biometrics, AI systems can provide immediate feedback, helping riders recognize when they are becoming stressed and offering tools to mitigate its effects. This proactive approach enables riders to manage stress before it negatively impacts their performance or mental health.

2. Stress Alerts and Intervention Suggestions

When AI identifies that a rider's stress levels are rising beyond optimal thresholds, it can send alerts in real-time. These alerts can be directly sent to the rider, their coach, or their medical team, prompting them to take action to lower stress levels. The AI system can suggest immediate interventions such as:

- **Breathing Exercises**: AI-powered apps can guide riders through short, structured breathing exercises designed to activate the parasympathetic nervous system, promoting relaxation and reducing anxiety.
- **Mindfulness or Meditation**: AI can recommend specific mindfulness or meditation sessions based on the rider's current stress profile. These sessions can be tailored to address anxiety, focus, or relaxation, depending on the rider's needs.
- **Rest Recommendations**: If stress levels are severely elevated, the AI system might suggest taking a break from practice or competition to allow the rider to recover mentally and physically. These recommendations can help prevent burnout and improve long-term performance.

In addition to real-time stress management, AI can also help riders understand their stress triggers over time. By tracking patterns in their physiological data, AI can identify common stressors—whether it's pre-race anxiety, post-crash tension, or fatigue during long rides—and recommend strategies for overcoming them.

AI Tools for Reducing Anxiety and Building Focus

Anxiety is a pervasive issue among athletes, and motocross riders are no exception. The fear of injury, performance pressure, and intense competition can all contribute to heightened anxiety, which can interfere with focus, decision-making, and overall performance. AI-powered tools are helping riders manage anxiety and build mental focus by providing personalized, data-driven strategies for anxiety reduction and concentration improvement.

1. Cognitive Behavioral Therapy (CBT) and AI

Cognitive Behavioral Therapy (CBT) is a highly effective psychological treatment for anxiety, as it helps individuals recognize and change negative thought patterns. AI is now being used to deliver elements of CBT to athletes, providing them with digital tools to manage anxiety. These tools are available through mobile apps and wearables, offering support whenever it's needed.

- **AI-Driven CBT Programs**: AI algorithms can be trained to provide personalized CBT sessions based on the rider's anxiety patterns. These sessions can help riders challenge irrational fears, reframe negative thoughts, and develop coping strategies for high-pressure situations. For example, if a rider experiences pre-race anxiety, the AI tool might suggest techniques for reframing negative thoughts and visualizing a successful race.
- **Automated Thought Record Keeping**: AI systems can prompt riders to track their thoughts and emotions throughout the day, helping them recognize patterns of anxiety. By analyzing this data, AI can offer insights into the underlying causes of anxiety and provide personalized coping strategies.

2. Focus and Mental Training Through AI

Motocross demands intense mental focus, especially during races where split-second decisions can make or break a performance. AI-powered tools are helping riders improve concentration and mental clarity, even under pressure.

- **Neurofeedback and Focus Training**: Some AI platforms use neurofeedback to help riders enhance their mental focus. These systems monitor brain activity in real time, providing feedback on how focused the rider is. AI can guide the rider through exercises to strengthen their concentration and improve mental resilience.
- **Personalized Mental Training Plans**: AI systems can create mental training regimens that include concentration exercises, visualization practices, and relaxation techniques designed to build focus and manage anxiety. These plans are tailored to the rider's individual needs and can be adjusted as they progress.

By reducing anxiety and building focus, AI tools help riders perform at their best during races, practice sessions, and recovery periods. These tools promote mental clarity and emotional stability, which are critical for achieving peak performance in the high-stakes world of motocross.

Long-Term Mental Wellness Planning

Maintaining mental health is not just about short-term interventions; it's about developing a long-term strategy for emotional well-being. AI systems are increasingly being used to create comprehensive mental wellness plans for riders, ensuring that they are not only recovering from injuries but also cultivating mental resilience over time.

1. Data-Driven Mental Health Planning

AI can integrate physical and psychological data to create a holistic wellness plan that includes both physical and mental health components. By tracking metrics such as stress levels, anxiety patterns, sleep quality, and mood, AI systems can help riders identify long-term trends and potential mental health challenges.

- **Integrated Wellness Reports**: AI can generate regular mental health reports that provide a summary of the rider's emotional and psychological status, highlighting any areas of concern. For example, if a rider has consistently low mood or high stress levels over several weeks, the system might suggest interventions such as therapy or changes in training schedules to reduce emotional strain.
- **Personalized Long-Term Strategies**: Based on data analysis, AI can help create personalized, long-term mental wellness strategies that include elements like stress management, work-life balance, and coping techniques for competition-related pressure.

2. Tracking Mental Health Progress

Mental health is an ongoing journey, and it's important for riders to track their emotional progress just as they track physical improvements. AI can provide tools for long-term mental health tracking, which helps ensure that riders stay on top of their psychological well-being.

- **Mood and Anxiety Journals**: Riders can use AI-powered apps to track their mood and anxiety levels daily. The AI system will analyze this data and highlight trends, enabling the rider to understand what factors are influencing their mental state and how they can adjust their training or lifestyle to improve it.
- **Adjusting Wellness Plans**: Over time, AI can adapt the rider's mental health plan based on their progress and changing needs. For instance, if a rider has successfully managed their anxiety for several months, the AI system might suggest new challenges to further enhance their mental resilience.

3. Encouraging Ongoing Mental Health Support

AI can also facilitate ongoing access to mental health support by connecting riders with mental health professionals, whether through virtual consultations or in-person appointments. These systems can offer riders regular check-ins, ensuring that they have a reliable support system in place for the long term.

- **Virtual Therapy**: AI-powered virtual therapy platforms can provide riders with easy access to counseling services, allowing them to talk to a licensed therapist remotely. These platforms can be integrated with AI systems that monitor the rider's emotional health, ensuring that they receive timely and appropriate support.

In summary, AI is playing a pivotal role in improving mental health support for motocross riders by providing tools to identify stress levels, reduce anxiety, enhance focus, and develop long-term wellness plans. By integrating AI with mental health strategies, riders can maintain emotional resilience and perform at their best both on and off the track. As the demands of the sport continue to evolve

Chapter 8: The Future of AI in Motocross

Section 1: Innovations on the Horizon

The landscape of motocross racing is evolving rapidly, driven in large part by advancements in technology. One of the most exciting and transformative developments is the integration of artificial intelligence (AI) in various aspects of the sport. From autonomous bikes to advanced robotics, AI is poised to revolutionize the way riders train, race, and recover. As AI continues to develop, the possibilities for the future of motocross are boundless, offering greater efficiency, enhanced safety, and personalized training experiences. In this section, we will explore the upcoming innovations in AI that are set to reshape the sport of motocross, focusing on advancements in autonomous bikes and robotics, the integration of AI with other cutting-edge technologies, and the future role of AI in coaching and training.

AI Advancements in Autonomous Bikes and Robotics

One of the most thrilling prospects in the future of motocross is the development of autonomous bikes. While the idea of autonomous vehicles has been a subject of research in the automotive industry for years, the application of this technology in extreme sports like motocross presents unique challenges and opportunities. AI's potential to create self-driving motorcycles is a game-changer, bringing innovations that could transform how races are conducted and how riders interact with their machines.

1. Autonomous Control Systems for Bikes

AI is already making strides in improving the control systems of motorcycles, and we are not far from seeing fully autonomous motorcycles designed for motocross tracks. These AI-powered systems would allow a bike to autonomously navigate the track, adjusting for terrain, speed, and obstacles in real time. Using machine learning algorithms, AI systems could continuously analyze data from sensors on the bike to improve the bike's ability to handle rough terrain, sharp turns, and jumps without direct input from the rider.

- **Advanced Sensors and Real-Time Data Processing**: Autonomous bikes will be equipped with a sophisticated network of sensors, including lidar, cameras, and gyroscopes, that will allow them to perceive and interact with their environment. These sensors will provide the bike with real-time data on the track's condition, terrain features, and obstacles. AI systems will then process this data and adjust the bike's throttle, suspension, and braking systems to ensure optimal performance.
- **AI-Based Learning and Adaptation**: One of the most exciting aspects of autonomous bikes is their ability to learn from experience. Through reinforcement learning, an AI-powered bike would be able to analyze past performance on various tracks and adapt its behavior accordingly. This could include optimizing speed during a corner, adjusting the suspension for different types of soil or bumps, or fine-tuning

power delivery for smoother acceleration. The bike would become increasingly skilled and efficient over time, pushing the boundaries of performance.

- **AI-Powered Safety Features**: Autonomous motorcycles could also integrate AI-driven safety features that predict and respond to potential risks. For example, AI could use data from sensors to detect obstacles or sudden changes in track conditions (like a wet patch or an unexpected turn) and automatically adjust the bike's behavior to prevent accidents. In high-risk environments like motocross, this type of real-time risk management could drastically reduce the number of crashes and improve rider safety.

While the idea of a fully autonomous motocross bike is still in its infancy, the groundwork being laid with AI-based control systems is already setting the stage for this exciting possibility. In the near future, autonomous bikes may not only be used in training and practice environments but could also be incorporated into competitive races, with AI managing the complexity of controlling the bike over challenging terrain.

2. Robotics for Maintenance and Support

Alongside the development of autonomous bikes, robotics will play an increasingly important role in supporting the sport of motocross, both on and off the track. Robotics can assist with various tasks, such as bike maintenance, rider recovery, and logistics. These innovations will improve efficiency and safety while allowing riders and teams to focus on performance.

- **Robot-Assisted Bike Maintenance**: Robotic systems, powered by AI, are being developed to assist with motorcycle maintenance and repairs. These robots can perform tasks such as tire changes, suspension adjustments, and engine diagnostics with high precision. This reduces downtime and ensures that bikes are always race-ready. AI-powered robots could also track the performance and wear-and-tear of different bike components, recommending maintenance actions before failures occur.
- **Robot-Assisted Rider Recovery**: Robotics can also support riders off the track, particularly when it comes to physical therapy and recovery. Exoskeletons and robotic rehabilitation devices are being integrated with AI systems to assist in injury recovery. These AI-driven devices can help riders recover faster by providing personalized movement patterns tailored to their specific injuries. For example, robotic exoskeletons can help rehabilitate a rider's legs by providing the necessary support to safely perform range-of-motion exercises, guided by AI.

The combination of autonomous bikes and robotics will fundamentally alter the role of the mechanic and support staff, making maintenance and recovery faster, safer, and more efficient.

Integrating AI with Other Cutting-Edge Technologies

AI is not functioning in isolation in the world of motocross; it is increasingly being integrated with other cutting-edge technologies to enhance the sport in novel ways. The convergence of AI, augmented reality (AR), virtual reality (VR), and big data analytics will create a highly immersive and data-driven future for motocross riders, teams, and fans. By combining AI with these technologies, the sport will become more dynamic, safer, and efficient.

1. Augmented Reality and AI for Rider Training

Augmented reality (AR) is one of the most exciting technologies being integrated with AI to enhance rider training and safety. AR systems overlay digital information onto the real-world environment, providing real-time insights and guidance. In the future, AI-powered AR systems could be used to guide motocross riders through training sessions, offering instant feedback on their riding techniques.

- **Real-Time Feedback**: By wearing AR glasses or using AR helmets, riders can receive real-time visual feedback on their performance. For example, if a rider is taking a corner too aggressively, the AR system could display an ideal line or recommend an adjustment. AI algorithms would analyze data from the rider's movements, speed, and trajectory to offer personalized suggestions for improvement.
- **Immersive Training Environments**: Using AI and AR together, riders could also train in virtual tracks, simulating various real-world environments and conditions. These virtual training sessions would allow riders to practice skills, like cornering and jumping, in a controlled but realistic setting. The AI system would monitor the rider's performance and make adjustments to the simulation, ensuring the rider gets the most out of each session.

2. Virtual Reality and AI for Race Simulation

Virtual reality (VR) is another technology that, when combined with AI, can take motocross training to the next level. VR simulations powered by AI can replicate actual race conditions, allowing riders to experience challenging tracks and terrains without leaving their training facility.

- **Race Simulation**: VR simulations can recreate a variety of race conditions, from different track layouts to varying weather conditions and even crowd noise. AI algorithms can adjust the simulation based on the rider's performance and provide dynamic feedback, helping the rider to prepare for a variety of scenarios they might face in real races.
- **Mental Preparation**: VR powered by AI can also be used to prepare riders mentally for the stress and pressure of real races. By simulating the experience of being at the starting line, in the midst of a race, or performing under intense competition, riders can practice mental focus, decision-making, and stress management techniques.

3. Big Data and AI for Performance Analysis

AI's ability to analyze and make sense of massive amounts of data is already transforming the world of motocross racing. Big data, when combined with AI, can provide insights that were previously unattainable. By tracking every aspect of a rider's performance, AI can help coaches and teams optimize training, race strategy, and overall performance.

- **Performance Analytics**: AI systems can analyze large datasets from sensors on bikes, wearable devices, and video cameras to assess a rider's performance. This data can include speed, heart rate, jump distance, cornering angle, and more. AI can then identify trends and areas of improvement, providing actionable insights that help riders fine-tune their training.

- **Predictive Analytics for Injury Prevention**: Big data combined with AI can be used to predict potential injuries before they happen. By analyzing historical data on rider behavior, track conditions, and injury occurrences, AI can identify risk factors and suggest modifications to training regimens or racing strategies to reduce the likelihood of injury.

The integration of AI with augmented reality, virtual reality, and big data will create a new era of training, performance optimization, and safety in motocross racing. These technologies will allow riders to train more efficiently, race smarter, and recover faster.

The Potential of AI in Motocross Coaching and Training

The future of AI in motocross is not just about smarter bikes and better technology—it's also about revolutionizing coaching and rider development. As AI continues to advance, it will offer new ways for coaches to train and mentor riders, providing a more personalized and data-driven approach to coaching.

- **AI-Powered Coaching Platforms**: AI-driven coaching platforms can analyze a rider's performance in real-time and provide coaches with detailed insights into their strengths and weaknesses. These platforms can also track a rider's progress over time, offering suggestions for improvement and adjusting training plans to meet their evolving needs.
- **Virtual Coaching**: As AI-powered virtual assistants and coaching platforms become more sophisticated, riders could receive personalized coaching virtually, reducing the need for constant in-person sessions. AI would act as a virtual coach, guiding riders through drills, offering tips, and providing motivation based on data-driven insights.

In the future, AI will play an indispensable role in shaping the next generation of motocross champions. By integrating AI with autonomous bikes, cutting-edge technologies, and personalized coaching methods, the sport will become faster, safer, and more accessible, with a deeper focus on optimizing both physical and mental performance.

As we look ahead, it is clear that the horizon for AI in motocross is full of endless possibilities, ushering in a new era of performance, safety, and innovation for riders at all levels.

Section 2: Preparing for the AI Revolution

As artificial intelligence (AI) continues to transform industries worldwide, motocross stands on the brink of its own AI revolution. Riders, teams, and stakeholders are being presented with unparalleled opportunities to integrate AI into training, bike optimization, and race strategies. However, this transformative period also brings unique challenges. To fully capitalize on AI's potential, motocross riders and teams must actively adapt, invest in relevant technologies, and address the hurdles that come with scaling AI solutions. This section explores how riders can embrace and learn AI tools, the opportunities for teams to invest in AI research, and strategies for overcoming challenges in adopting AI at scale.

How Riders Can Embrace and Learn AI Tools

The key to thriving in an AI-driven motocross era lies in the willingness of riders to embrace new tools and technologies. These tools can improve their performance, increase safety, and provide data-driven insights into their training and racing routines.

1. Educating Riders on AI Fundamentals

For many riders, the concept of AI may seem distant or overly complex. However, a basic understanding of how AI functions can help them recognize its potential and use it effectively.

- **Workshops and Training Programs**: Riders should participate in workshops and training sessions focused on AI applications in motocross. These could cover topics like AI-powered wearable devices, analytics platforms, and virtual coaching systems.
- **User-Friendly Tools**: Many AI tools are designed to be intuitive, requiring minimal technical expertise. Riders can start with simpler tools, such as fitness tracking apps or bike diagnostic platforms, before progressing to more complex systems like predictive analytics.
- **Collaborative Learning**: Riders can benefit from collaborating with teams and coaches who are already familiar with AI. Peer learning and shared experiences can demystify AI tools, making them more accessible.

2. Leveraging Wearables and Real-Time Data

One of the easiest ways for riders to integrate AI into their routines is through wearable devices. These devices provide valuable insights into physical performance and riding techniques.

- **Performance Metrics**: Wearable sensors can track data like heart rate, oxygen levels, and muscle fatigue. AI systems analyze this data to recommend training adjustments that enhance endurance and reduce the risk of injury.
- **Riding Analytics**: Riders can use AI tools to analyze their riding posture, cornering techniques, and jump execution. This information helps them identify areas for improvement and refine their skills.
- **Customizable Goals**: Many AI tools allow riders to set specific goals, such as improving lap times or mastering certain track sections. The system provides tailored feedback and progress tracking, ensuring consistent growth.

3. Developing a Growth Mindset Toward AI Integration

Embracing AI requires a shift in mindset. Riders must view AI as a partner that enhances their skills rather than a replacement for their expertise.

- **Balancing Intuition and Data**: While AI provides valuable insights, motocross racing still requires instinct and experience. Riders should use AI as a supplement to their decision-making, not a substitute.
- **Continuous Learning**: The AI landscape is constantly evolving, with new tools and updates being introduced regularly. Riders who commit to lifelong learning will stay ahead of the curve and maximize their competitive edge.

Opportunities for Teams to Invest in AI Research

Teams play a critical role in driving AI adoption in motocross. By investing in AI research and infrastructure, teams can gain a significant competitive advantage while shaping the future of the sport.

1. Partnering with Technology Developers

One of the most effective ways for teams to integrate AI is by partnering with technology developers who specialize in AI solutions for sports.

- **Collaborative Development**: Teams can collaborate with AI developers to create custom tools tailored to their specific needs. For example, a team could work on creating a suspension optimization system that adjusts to different track conditions in real time.
- **Beta Testing**: Teams that partner with tech companies can act as beta testers for new AI products. This allows them to access cutting-edge technology before it becomes widely available, giving them a competitive edge.
- **Feedback Loops**: By providing feedback to developers, teams can influence the design and functionality of AI tools, ensuring they align with the practical demands of motocross racing.

2. Building AI Research Divisions

Larger teams with substantial resources can establish dedicated AI research divisions focused on innovation and performance optimization.

- **Data Science Teams**: These divisions could employ data scientists and AI specialists who analyze race data, rider performance metrics, and bike diagnostics. The insights generated by these experts can inform strategic decisions and long-term planning.
- **AI-Driven Experimentation**: Research divisions could conduct experiments to test the effectiveness of different AI systems, such as predictive maintenance tools or virtual training environments. The results of these experiments could help teams identify the most impactful technologies.

- **Knowledge Sharing**: Research findings could be shared with other departments within the team, fostering a culture of innovation and collaboration.

3. Sponsorship and Funding Opportunities

Teams can also explore sponsorship and funding opportunities related to AI research.

- **AI Sponsorships**: Partnering with AI companies as sponsors not only provides financial support but also grants access to cutting-edge technologies.
- **Grants and Investments**: Many organizations and governments offer grants for sports technology research. Teams can leverage these opportunities to fund their AI initiatives.

Challenges and Solutions in Adopting AI at Scale

Despite its potential, adopting AI in motocross comes with its own set of challenges. Teams and riders must address these obstacles to ensure a smooth transition into the AI era.

1. High Costs of AI Implementation

One of the most significant barriers to AI adoption is the high cost of acquiring and implementing AI systems. From purchasing advanced sensors to hiring data specialists, the financial burden can be substantial.

- **Solution: Phased Implementation**: Teams can adopt AI in phases, starting with low-cost tools like performance tracking apps before moving on to more expensive systems like predictive analytics.
- **Pooling Resources**: Smaller teams can collaborate and pool resources to share the cost of AI tools and research.
- **Leveraging Open-Source Tools**: Many AI tools and frameworks are available as open-source software, providing a cost-effective way to get started.

2. Resistance to Change

Some riders and teams may be hesitant to adopt AI, fearing it will diminish traditional skills or disrupt established routines.

- **Solution: Education and Awareness**: Organizing workshops and informational sessions can help stakeholders understand the benefits of AI and address their concerns.
- **Demonstrating ROI**: Sharing success stories and case studies that highlight the tangible benefits of AI can help overcome resistance.

3. Data Privacy and Security

AI systems rely heavily on data, raising concerns about privacy and security. Riders and teams may worry about sensitive information being leaked or misused.

- **Solution: Robust Security Measures**: Implementing secure data storage and encryption protocols can protect sensitive information.
- **Transparency and Consent**: Teams should be transparent about how data is collected and used, ensuring riders give informed consent.

4. Technical Expertise

Many teams lack the technical expertise needed to implement and manage AI systems effectively.

- **Solution: Upskilling and Hiring**: Teams can invest in training programs to upskill their existing staff or hire experts in AI and data analytics.
- **Partnering with Specialists**: Collaborating with technology providers or consultants can fill knowledge gaps and ensure successful implementation.

Preparing for the AI revolution in motocross requires proactive efforts from both riders and teams. Riders must embrace AI tools as a means to enhance their performance, while teams must invest in research and innovation to stay competitive. By addressing challenges like cost, resistance to change, and data security, the motocross community can unlock the full potential of AI. As the sport evolves, those who adapt to the AI revolution will not only thrive but also shape the future of motocross. With careful planning and a forward-thinking mindset, the possibilities are limitless.

Section 3: Vision for AI-Driven Motocross

As artificial intelligence (AI) reshapes industries worldwide, the future of motocross holds incredible potential for transformation. AI's integration into motocross promises to revolutionize the experience for riders, fans, and stakeholders by enhancing performance, fostering collaboration, and creating innovative opportunities. This vision for an AI-driven motocross world revolves around three key pillars: reimagining the experience for riders and fans, creating a collaborative AI ecosystem within the industry, and building the AI-powered motocross world of tomorrow.

Reimagining the Motocross Experience for Riders and Fans

Motocross is a high-intensity sport where speed, precision, and passion collide. AI has the potential to take the experience to new heights, not only for riders striving to perfect their performance but also for fans seeking deeper engagement.

1. Personalizing the Rider Experience

AI can tailor training and racing experiences to meet the unique needs of each rider, enabling them to push their limits and achieve peak performance.

- **Custom Training Regimens**: Using data from wearable devices and track analytics, AI can create personalized training programs that address a rider's strengths and weaknesses. These dynamic plans evolve based on progress and real-time feedback.
- **Adaptive Racing Strategies**: AI-powered tools can provide riders with insights into track conditions, competitor performance, and optimal racing lines during a race, allowing them to adapt their strategies for maximum impact.
- **Real-Time Coaching**: AI systems equipped with voice assistants could deliver instant feedback to riders during training sessions, offering advice on technique and helping them correct mistakes on the spot.

2. Enhancing Fan Engagement

For fans, AI has the potential to bring motocross to life in ways that were previously unimaginable, transforming passive spectators into active participants.

- **Immersive Virtual Experiences**: AI-powered virtual and augmented reality (VR/AR) platforms could allow fans to experience races from a rider's perspective, complete with live telemetry and commentary.
- **AI-Enhanced Broadcasts**: During live broadcasts, AI can provide real-time data overlays, such as rider speeds, lap times, and predictions for race outcomes, enhancing viewers' understanding of the action.
- **Interactive Fan Platforms**: AI-driven apps and platforms could let fans predict race results, interact with riders through virtual meet-and-greets, and even compete in virtual races using real-world data from the track.

3. Expanding Accessibility

AI can make motocross more accessible to individuals who may not have had the opportunity to participate in or follow the sport before.

- **Affordable Training Simulators**: Virtual training systems powered by AI could enable aspiring riders to practice and hone their skills in a safe, cost-effective environment.
- **Global Fan Connectivity**: AI can connect fans worldwide through multilingual content, interactive communities, and social media analytics, fostering a truly global motocross community.

Creating a Collaborative AI Ecosystem in the Industry

The successful integration of AI in motocross will depend on collaboration between various stakeholders, including riders, teams, manufacturers, event organizers, and technology developers. Building a robust AI ecosystem requires a shared commitment to innovation and mutual growth.

1. Strengthening Partnerships Between Teams and Tech Companies

Collaboration between motocross teams and AI developers is essential for designing tools and systems that meet the sport's unique demands.

- **Joint Innovation Initiatives**: Teams and tech companies can work together to develop custom solutions, such as advanced suspension systems, real-time analytics platforms, or AI-driven diagnostics tools.
- **Knowledge Exchange**: Sharing expertise between the motocross and tech industries can accelerate the development of groundbreaking technologies and ensure that they are practical and effective.
- **Beta Testing and Feedback Loops**: Riders and teams can act as beta testers for new AI tools, providing valuable feedback to refine and improve these systems before they are launched commercially.

2. Fostering Collaboration Across the Motocross Ecosystem

AI can act as a unifying force, bringing together different players within the motocross industry to work toward common goals.

- **Standardizing Data Sharing**: Establishing standardized protocols for collecting and sharing data can enable teams, manufacturers, and event organizers to collaborate more effectively.
- **Creating Shared Platforms**: Centralized AI platforms could allow teams to access track analytics, rider performance data, and competitor insights, fostering a spirit of healthy competition.
- **Industry-Wide Research Initiatives**: Collective investments in AI research and development can drive innovation and benefit all stakeholders in the motocross ecosystem.

3. Emphasizing Ethics and Fairness

As AI becomes more prevalent, it is crucial to address ethical considerations and ensure that its use promotes fairness and integrity in the sport.

- **Transparency in AI Algorithms**: Ensuring that AI systems are transparent and explainable can build trust among riders, teams, and fans.
- **Regulating AI Usage**: Governing bodies must establish clear guidelines for how AI can be used in training, bike optimization, and race strategy to maintain a level playing field.
- **Promoting Inclusivity**: AI tools should be designed to be accessible and affordable for teams and riders of all levels, preventing a technology gap from widening disparities in the sport.

Building the AI-Powered Motocross World of Tomorrow

The future of motocross lies in leveraging AI to push the boundaries of what is possible, creating a sport that is faster, safer, and more thrilling than ever before.

1. The Role of Autonomous Bikes and Robotics

While motocross will always be a rider-centric sport, advancements in autonomous vehicles and robotics could play a significant role in its future.

- **Self-Learning Bikes**: AI-powered bikes equipped with self-learning algorithms could adapt to track conditions and rider inputs, optimizing performance in real time.
- **Safety Robotics**: Autonomous drones and robots could be deployed during races to monitor safety conditions, provide emergency assistance, and ensure rider well-being.
- **AI-Driven Testing**: Robotics could be used for testing new equipment and track designs, providing valuable data without putting riders at risk.

2. Integrating AI with Other Technologies

AI's potential can be further amplified by integrating it with other cutting-edge technologies, such as IoT, 5G, and blockchain.

- **Smart Equipment**: Internet of Things (IoT)-enabled bikes and gear could communicate with AI systems to provide seamless, real-time updates on performance and safety.
- **High-Speed Connectivity**: The rollout of 5G networks will enable faster data transfer between AI systems, enhancing their ability to deliver instant insights and recommendations.
- **Secure Data Management**: Blockchain technology could ensure the secure storage and sharing of sensitive data, such as rider analytics and race results.

3. Inspiring the Next Generation

AI-driven innovations can inspire the next generation of riders, engineers, and fans to engage with motocross in new and exciting ways.

- **Youth Training Programs**: AI-powered simulators and virtual coaches could introduce young riders to motocross, helping them develop skills and confidence before hitting the track.
- **STEM Education**: The intersection of AI and motocross can serve as a powerful tool for promoting STEM (science, technology, engineering, and mathematics) education, inspiring students to pursue careers in sports technology.
- **Global Outreach**: By making motocross more accessible and engaging, AI can help expand the sport's reach to new audiences and regions, fostering a diverse and inclusive community.

The vision for an AI-driven motocross world is one of limitless potential. By reimagining the experience for riders and fans, creating a collaborative ecosystem within the industry, and embracing cutting-edge innovations, motocross can achieve unprecedented levels of performance, safety, and engagement. As AI continues to evolve, its integration into motocross will not only transform the sport but also inspire a new generation of riders, fans, and innovators to dream big and push the boundaries of what is possible. The future of motocross is bright, and AI is the key to unlocking its full potential.

Conclusion: The New Frontier of Motocross with AI

Motocross, a sport defined by its adrenaline-fueled races, relentless challenges, and unyielding passion, stands on the brink of a groundbreaking transformation. As artificial intelligence (AI) continues to reshape industries around the world, its integration into motocross has the power to redefine every aspect of the sport, from training and performance optimization to safety, race management, and fan engagement. This book has explored the vast opportunities AI presents, along with its potential to create a smarter, safer, and more exciting motocross world for riders, teams, and enthusiasts alike.

Revolutionizing Rider Training and Performance

At the heart of motocross is the rider, and AI has the ability to unlock their full potential in unprecedented ways. Through wearable technology, AI-driven analytics, and virtual coaching systems, riders can receive personalized feedback, enhance their physical and mental resilience, and continually adapt to new challenges. AI tools like simulation-based training environments and machine learning insights have opened doors to highly efficient, data-driven skill development.

Injury prevention and recovery are also undergoing a revolution. Wearable devices and predictive algorithms help riders avoid risks and recover faster after injuries, while mental health tools use AI to address stress, anxiety, and long-term wellness. These advancements ensure riders are not only physically prepared but also mentally fortified for the demands of this high-stakes sport.

Pushing the Boundaries of Bike Performance

A motocross bike is more than just a machine—it's a rider's partner on the track. AI is enhancing this relationship by offering smarter diagnostic systems, predictive maintenance tools, and real-time customization options. From optimizing suspension settings to adjusting engine performance based on terrain and weather conditions, AI enables riders to push their machines to new limits with precision and confidence.

Safety remains a top priority, and AI is stepping in with crash prediction technologies, real-time alerts for potential hazards, and enhanced monitoring systems for both rider and bike. These advancements ensure that motocross continues to be thrilling while reducing the risks inherent in the sport.

Redefining Track Analysis and Strategy

The track is the ultimate test of a rider's skill and a bike's capability. AI offers tools to map and analyze track dynamics with incredible accuracy, giving riders and teams a significant strategic edge. Drones and AI-driven sensors collect data on track surfaces, weather conditions, and competitor movements, enabling riders to adapt their racing lines and strategies dynamically.

Post-race analytics have never been more comprehensive. AI-generated reports highlight areas for improvement, empowering riders to refine their skills and teams to develop better race plans. This data-driven approach ensures that motocross is not just a sport of instinct but also one of intelligence.

Enhancing the Spectator and Fan Experience

AI is bringing motocross closer to fans, creating immersive experiences that engage audiences on a deeper level. Virtual and augmented reality allow fans to experience races from a rider's perspective, while AI-driven broadcasting and interactive platforms offer real-time insights and analysis during events. These technologies transform spectators into active participants, making the sport more accessible and engaging than ever before.

AI also strengthens the connection between riders and their fans, fostering a sense of community that transcends the boundaries of the track. By integrating fan-driven insights, AI ensures that motocross remains a sport for everyone, whether they're cheering from the stands or watching from across the globe.

Shaping the Future of Motocross

The future of motocross lies in its ability to embrace and adapt to the rapid advancements in AI technology. Emerging trends such as autonomous bikes, robotics, and the integration of AI with Internet of Things (IoT) devices will continue to push the sport into uncharted territory. However, these innovations also come with challenges, from ethical considerations to the need for clear regulations and guidelines.

By fostering collaboration across teams, manufacturers, and technology providers, motocross can build an AI-powered ecosystem that promotes innovation, fairness, and inclusivity. Investment in AI research and development will not only give teams a competitive edge but also ensure that the sport remains sustainable and environmentally conscious.

Motocross: Powered by Passion and Intelligence

At its core, motocross is a celebration of human determination, mechanical ingenuity, and the thrill of competition. AI does not diminish these qualities; instead, it enhances them by providing tools and insights that allow riders, teams, and fans to experience motocross like never before.

This book has illuminated the incredible possibilities that AI offers, from revolutionizing rider training and bike performance to redefining race strategies and fan engagement. The journey ahead is one of continuous learning and adaptation, but the rewards are well worth the effort. AI has the power to make motocross safer, smarter, and more exhilarating, ensuring its legacy as one of the most dynamic sports in the world.

As we look to the future, the integration of AI into motocross is not just a technological advancement—it's a testament to the sport's ability to evolve and inspire. With AI as a trusted partner, the possibilities are limitless, and the track is wide open for riders, teams, and fans to explore this exciting new frontier together. The revolution has begun, and the future of motocross has never been brighter.

www.ingramcontent.com/pod-product-compliance
Lightning Source LLC
LaVergne TN
LVHW022354060326
832902LV00022B/4433